Paper Plate Arts and Crafts Activities

Week-by-Week Projects Using Paper Plates

by Julie and Thomas McKenzie

illustrated by Veronica Terrill

Teaching & Learning Company

1204 Buchanan St., P.O. Box 10
Carthage, IL 62321

Cover photo by Images and More Photography

Copyright © 1996, Teaching & Learning Company

ISBN No. 1-57310-039-0

Printing No. 98765432

Teaching & Learning Company
1204 Buchanan St., P.O. Box 10
Carthage, IL 62321

This book belongs to

_____

Table of Contents

February

March

April

May

Summer

General

Dear Teacher or Parent,

When it comes to making craft projects out of paper plates, it may seem as if there is not much new under (and including) the sun . . . UNTIL NOW!

Here is a totally unique approach to paper plate art activities. Say good-bye to standby smiley face masks and boring bookworms, and bring on the triceratops, Cinco de Mayo shakers, Kwanzaa candelabras and touchdown toys! Celebrate Columbus with a tabletop display, Chinese New Year with a dragon puppet and welcome the swallows back to Capistrano with a soaring mobile.

There are four weekly activities for each month. You can use use one per week or pick and choose items to fit into your own curriculum. Literature suggestions that relate to the topic are given for each project. The literature can be used to broaden the children's knowledge and demonstrate a connection between literature and learning.

For each activity, you'll find clear, easy-to-follow directions. The steps are illustrated for clarity and some include reproducible patterns which you can copy for as many students as needed. The "Tips and Suggestions" section provides some general information and helpful hints. A reproducible letter to parents requests supplies needed to complete the projects.

We hope you and your children will find the projects in this book unique and exciting, and that your finished products will represent a fun and memorable learning experience.

Enjoy!

Sincerely,

Julie   Thomas

Julie and Thomas McKenzie

Tips and Suggestions

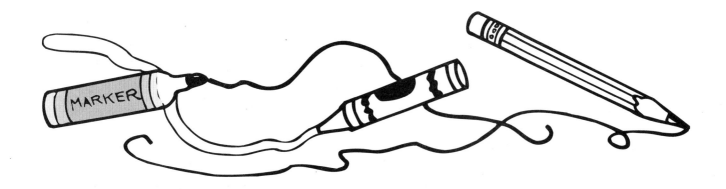

We have used 6" (15 cm) and 9" (23 cm) paper plates to fashion the crafts in this book.

Make a sample of the craft before it is presented. You will be better prepared to answer questions, and students may refer to it as a guide for their creations.

You may need to show your students how to make certain forms such as cones, cylinders, tubes, etc.

If necessary (due to age, time or physical limitation), you may wish to provide your students with templates to trace patterns onto the plates they will be cutting. You might also wish to provide some preassembled components.

Provide your classroom with a scrap bag. Place useable scraps in the bag after each project. The scraps may come in handy for a future craft. This not only helps you keep costs at a minimum, it is also a lesson in recycling.

You may want to set aside class time on two consecutive days instead of trying to complete some of the more involved crafts in just one session.

Preprinted plates can be used on some of the projects to save time.

Markers and crayons work best to color the paper plates. You might want to experiment with colored pencils, tempera paints, watercolors or other coloring media. Not all paint adheres well to all types of paper plates.

Use craft glue, tacky glue or white glue. Paste is not recommended. Remember, a little glue goes a long way! A dab of glue and a squeeze for a few seconds are good techniques.

Tips and Suggestions

Create fringe as follows:

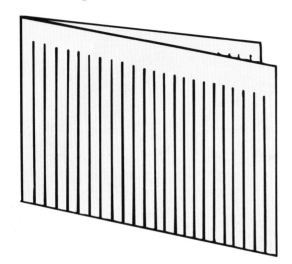

For grass, cut fringe pieces as thin as you can and gently push apart.

Fringe can easily be curled between your thumb and index finger.

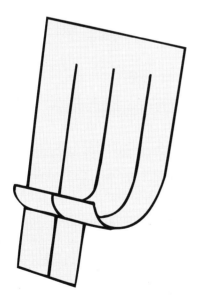

Pedestals can be made as follows:

paper cube

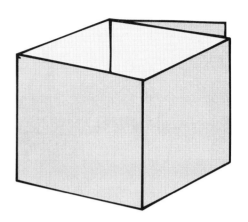

paper spring

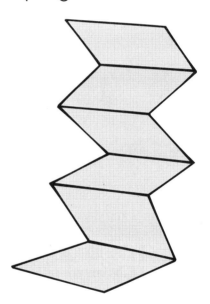

sponge cube

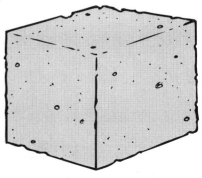

Tips and Suggestions

The following illustrations may clarify
some of the directions:

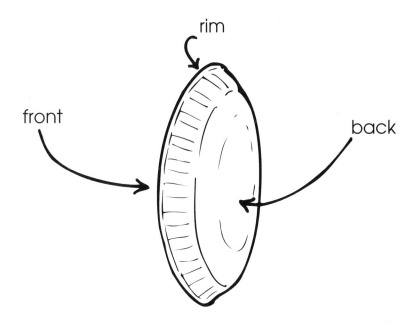

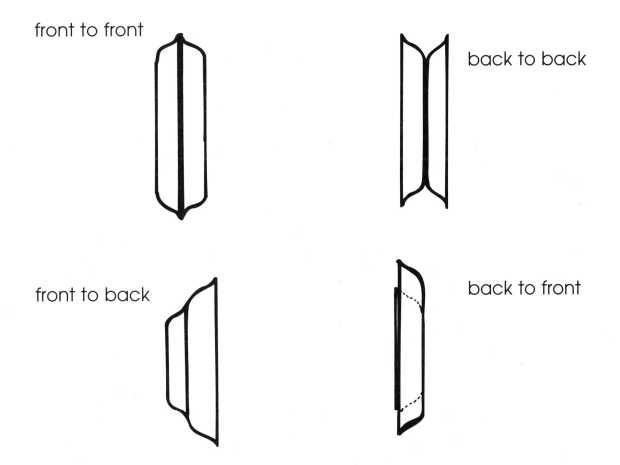

Dear Parent,

We will be working on craft projects that utilize paper plates. These creative activities give your child the opportunity to practice skills (listening, following directions, motor coordination), engage in self-expression and enjoy the process of constructing an item that can be admired by family and friends.

I hope you will encourage your child's efforts in this–and in all areas of his or her schoolwork–and I also hope that you might be able to contribute some of the following materials (checked items, please):

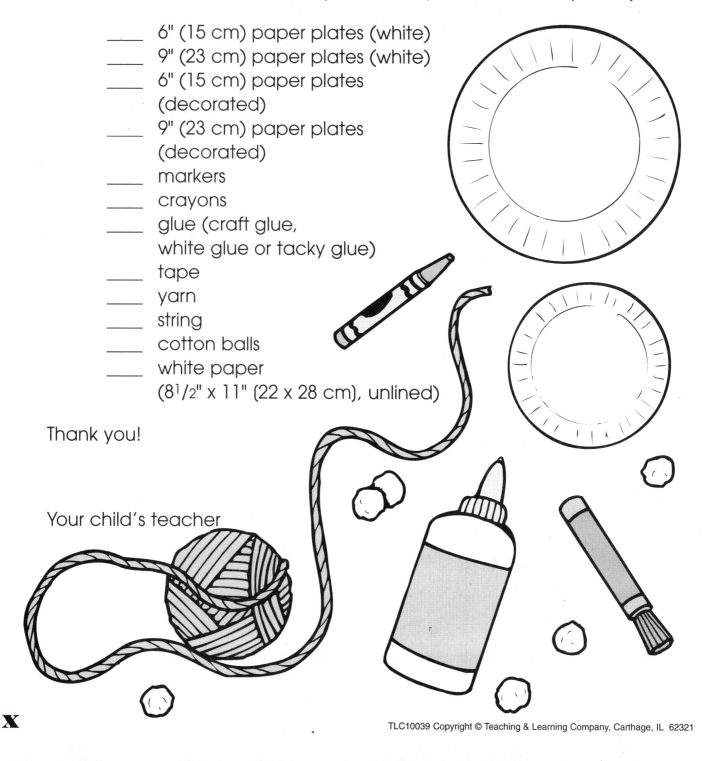

____ 6" (15 cm) paper plates (white)
____ 9" (23 cm) paper plates (white)
____ 6" (15 cm) paper plates (decorated)
____ 9" (23 cm) paper plates (decorated)
____ markers
____ crayons
____ glue (craft glue, white glue or tacky glue)
____ tape
____ yarn
____ string
____ cotton balls
____ white paper (8$\frac{1}{2}$" x 11" (22 x 28 cm), unlined)

Thank you!

Your child's teacher

X

Welcome Back to School

Materials

one 9" paper plate
two 6" paper plates
copy paper (any color)
markers or crayons
scissors
glue

Directions

1. Before your students arrive, copy the words *Welcome Back to School* (see page 3) on a piece of paper. Make one copy for each student.

2. Ask the students to cut out the words and set aside. The letters can be colored before they are cut out.

3. Glue a 6" plate facedown to the middle front of a 9" plate.

4. Glue the words around the outside front rim of the 9" plate.

5. Have each student draw a self-portrait in the middle of a 6" plate and write his name under the drawing.

6. Glue the back of the self-portrait plate to the 6" plate.

Variations

1. Use a 9" preprinted plate for the background.

2. Ask the students to write *Welcome Back to School* around the rim of the 9" plate instead of cutting out the letters.

Literature Selection

School
by Emily Arnold McCully
Harper & Row, 1987

Selected Activity

Hang this project on the front of the students' desks for the first week to help with name recognition.

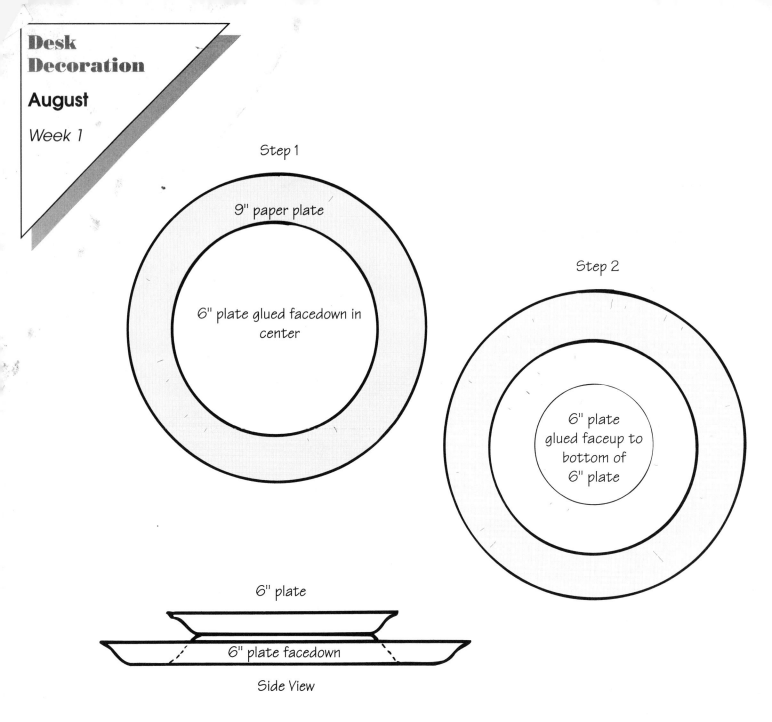

Step 1

9" paper plate

6" plate glued facedown in center

Step 2

6" plate glued faceup to bottom of 6" plate

6" plate

6" plate facedown

Side View

Extended Activity

Instead of having children draw their own portraits, ask them to work in pairs and draw each other. This is a great getting-to-know-you exercise.

Note

See page 3 for letter patterns to be used with this activity.

WELCOME BACK TO SCHOOL

Flying High

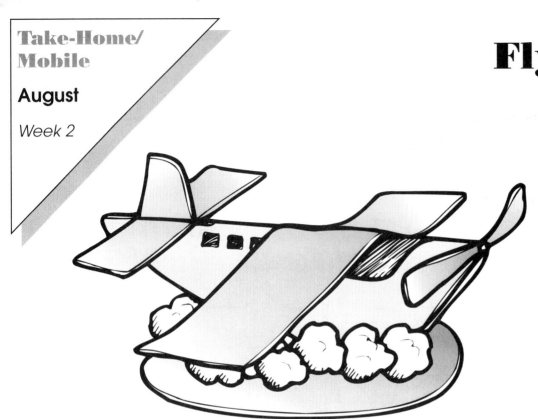

Materials

two 9" paper plates
one 6" paper plate
markers or crayons
cotton balls
scissors
glue

Directions

1. Color the back of the 6" plate to resemble sky. Set aside.

2. Fold one of the 9" plates in half to represent the body of the plane. Cut out the airplane body and color. Glue the bottom of the body to the 6" plate.

3. Color and cut out large wings, propellers, tail and tail wings from the other 9" plate. See cutting guidelines on page 5. Use the patterns provided on page 6. Glue the tail into the slit on the short end of the body. Glue the tail wings on either side of the tail. Glue the propellers onto the end of the nose. Glue the wings onto the midsection of the body at the fold.

4. Glue cotton balls around the plane to make it look like it is flying through the clouds.

5. Decorate the body and wings with colorful stickers.

Literature Selection

Snoopy's Facts and Fun Book About Planes
Random House, 1979

Selected Activity

This project can be used as part of a social studies, math or a history curriculum.

Extended Activity

Children will enjoy taking this project home and displaying it for friends and family. If you eliminate the 6" base plate, you can hang the airplane from the ceiling for an attractive mobile. Use varying lengths of string to hang many airplanes.

4

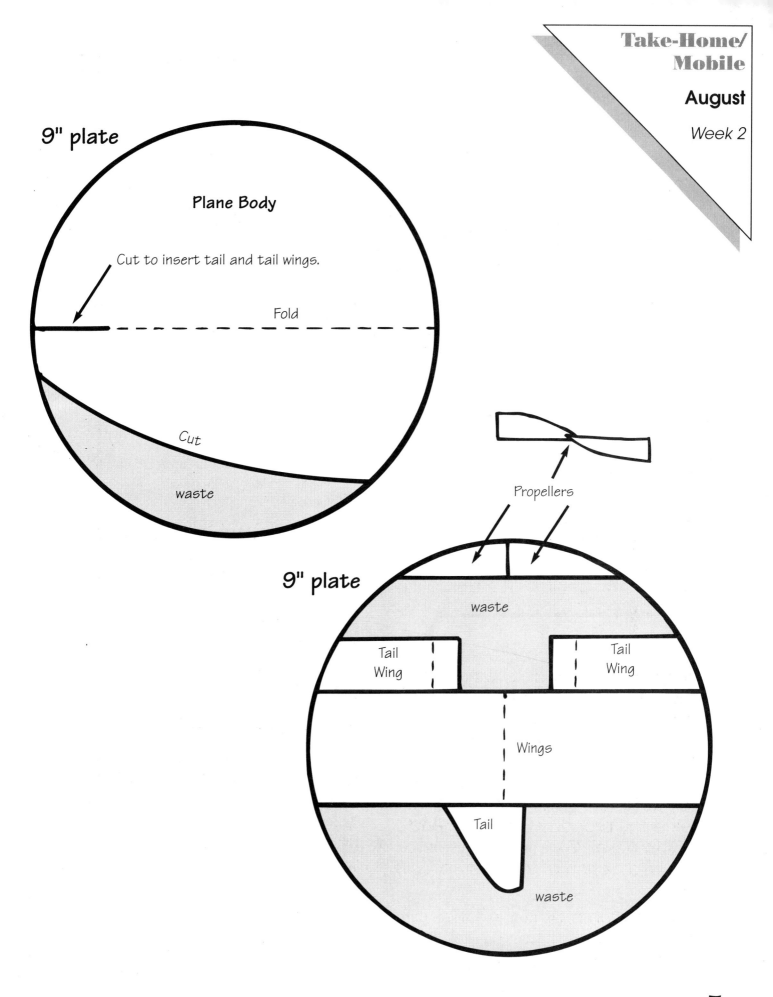

9" plate

Plane Body

Cut to insert tail and tail wings.

Fold

Cut

waste

Propellers

9" plate

waste

Tail
Wing

Tail
Wing

Wings

Tail

waste

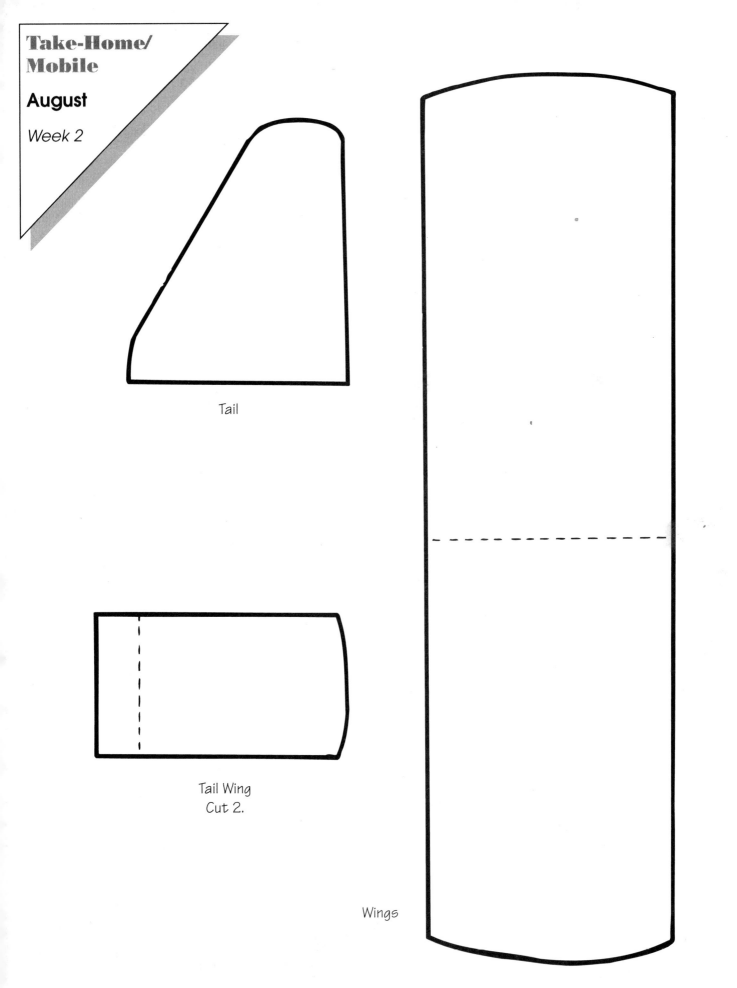

Tail

Tail Wing
Cut 2.

Wings

UFO Thrower

Materials

two 9" paper plates
two 6" paper plates
markers or crayons
glue

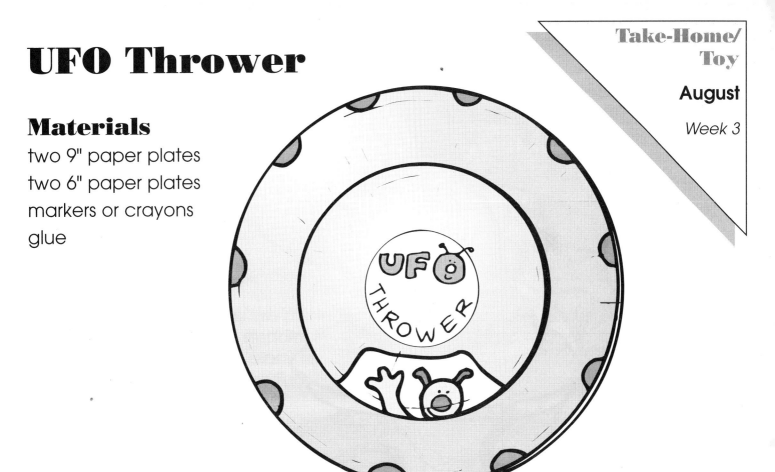

Directions

1. Color the backs of the two 9" and the two 6" plates to resemble a UFO. Use any design and colors that you like.

2. Glue the two 9" plates together, front to front.

3. Glue the 6" plates, front side down, to the outside middles of the 9" plates.

4. Let the glue dry and toss like a flying disk–they will soar far!

Literature Selection

Space Case
by Edward Marshall
Dial, 1980

Variation

Use stickers or construction paper cut-outs to decorate the throwers.

Selected Activity

This project can be used as a part of a science or math curriculum. Have children measure the distances their UFO Throwers have travelled. Compare on a chart or graph.

Extended Activity

Design a course for the Throwers. See who can complete it in the fewest number of tosses.

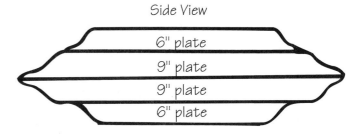

Side View

6" plate
9" plate
9" plate
6" plate

7

Plato the Frog

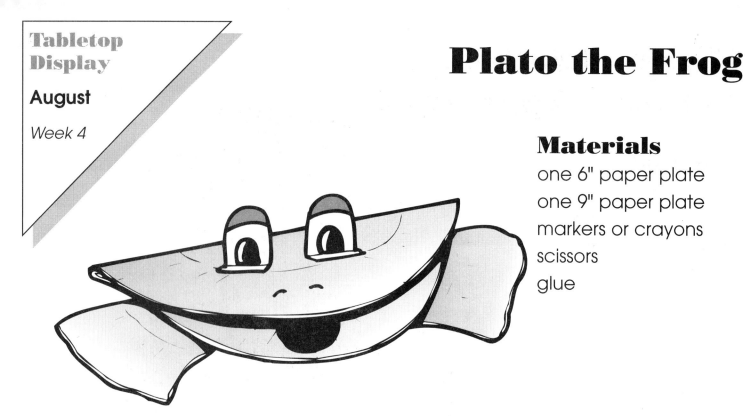

Materials

one 6" paper plate
one 9" paper plate
markers or crayons
scissors
glue

Directions

1. Color the back of the 6" plate green, color the front pink and draw a tongue facing out toward the rim on one half.

2. Fold the plate in half (with the tongue on the bottom), place a dot of glue near the fold at each corner and pinch closed.

3. Color half of the bottom of the 9" plate green. Cut out and cut in half to make two wide triangles. Glue the pointed ends of these triangles to the bottom of the folded plate to make the feet.

4. Cut two U-shaped eye pieces out of the white scraps from the 9" plate. Draw on pupils and fold the bottom up approximately 1/4" (.6 cm). Glue these folds to the top of the 6" plate to make the eyes. (Make sure that the eyes stand up.)

Variation

Make a lily pad from a 9" plate for the frog to sit on. A fly can be made from plate scraps to land on the frog's tongue.

Literature Selections

The Princess and the Froggie
by Harve and Kathe Zemach
Farrar Strauss and Giroux, 1975

Tiddalick the Frog
by Susan Nunes
Atheneum, 1989

Selected Activity

This project can be used as a part of a science curriculum.

Extended Activity

Cover a tabletop or bulletin board with blue paper. Place the frogs and lily pads on the "pond" for a display.

8

Happy Birthday, Johnny Appleseed

Materials

four 9" paper plates
one 6" paper plate
markers or crayons
scissors
glue

Directions

1. Write the words *Happy Birthday, Johnny Appleseed* onto the back rim of a 9" plate.

2. Color the back of the 6" plate green and glue, front to back, to the middle of the 9" plate.

3. From the three remaining 9" plates, cut three tree forms. See the template for these on page 10. Color one side of the tree forms to look like an apple tree.

4. Fold the tree forms in half, open slightly and glue the fold lines back to back to form a full, three-dimensional tree.

5. Fold up the bottom of the trunk about 1/4" (.6 cm) to make tabs. Glue the tree to the center of the 6" plate.

Literature Selection

Johnny Appleseed
by Steven Kellogg
Morrow Junior Books, 1988

Selected Activity

Using the pattern on page 10, make apples from construction paper to glue on the trees. Write a number or a math problem on the base plate. Children must glue that number of apples onto the tree.

Place this edge on outer rim of 9" plate.

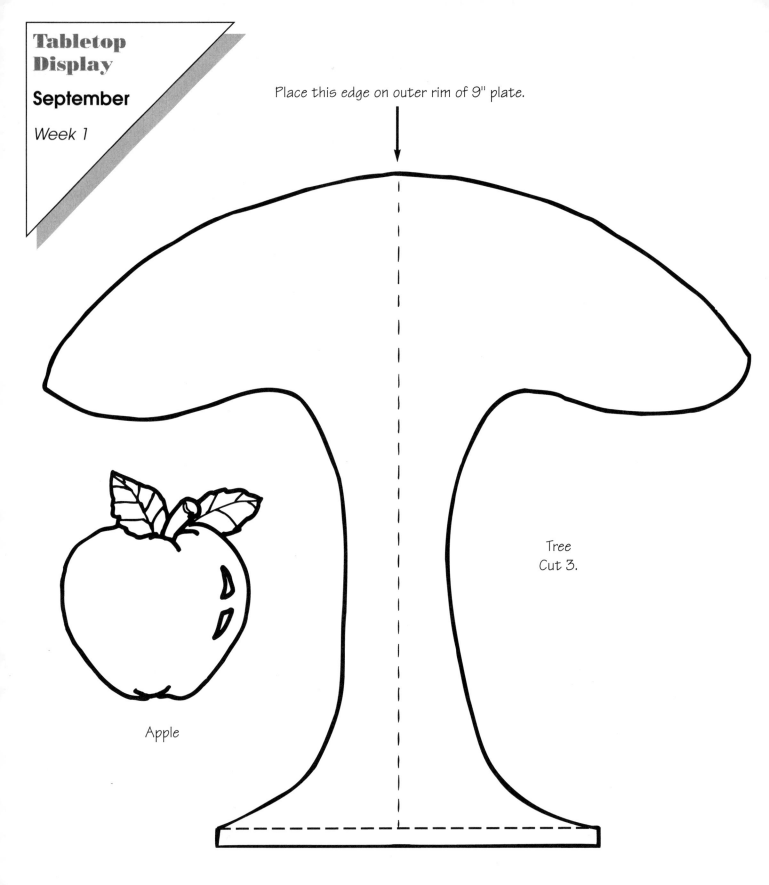

Tree
Cut 3.

Apple

Best Grandparent Award

Materials

two 6" paper plates
one 9" paper plate
markers or crayons
scissors
glue

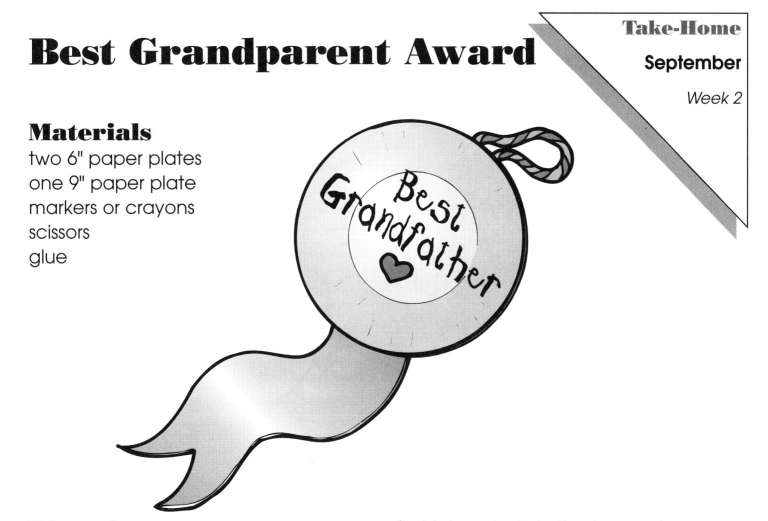

Directions

1. Cut a ribbon shape approximately 5¹/₂" (14 cm) long from the middle of the 9" paper plate. Cut a "V" into one end. Color the ribbon.

2. Glue the ribbon to the bottom front of a 6" plate. Make sure that the "V" end is hanging down.

3. Color the back of the remaining 6" plate. Across the middle, write a phrase like: Best Grandmother, Best Grandfather, #1 Grandma, etc.

Variations

1. Children can make an award for each grandparent.

2. Put potpourri in between the plates and poke small holes in the back to release the fragrance.

3. Make a hole in the top and thread a piece of yarn through to make a necklace.

4. Actual ribbon can be used in place of the paper plate ribbon.

Literature Selections

Abuela
by Arthur Dorros
Dutton, 1991

When I Am Old with You
by Angela Johnson
Orchard Books, 1990

Selected Activity

Invite grandparents to class for a snack and to receive their awards.

11

Silly Ears

Materials

two 9" paper plates
two 6" paper plates
markers or crayons
scissors
glue

Directions

1. Color the 9" plates in the design of your choosing. After coloring, cut the plates in half.

2. Color the two 6" plates. Glue the back of each 6" plate to the front center of each 9" plate half. Let the glue dry.

3. Cut ear holes out of the centers and slip over the ears.

Variation

If you are short on time, use preprinted paper plates.

Literature Selections

Ear Book
by Al Perkins
Random, 1968

Ears Are for Hearing
by Paul Showers
HarperCollins, 1993

Listen Up! Math
Listen Up! Science
Listen Up! Language Arts
by Ann Richmond Fisher
Teaching & Learning Company, 1994

Selected Activity

Have your students wear their ears during story time or any other time when it is important that they listen.

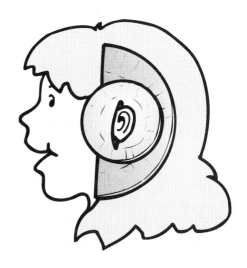

Pumpkin Carriage

Materials

two 9" paper plates
five 6" paper plates
markers or crayons
scissors
glue

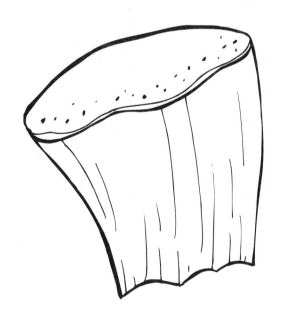

Directions

1. Color the backs of the two 9" plates to look like pumpkins. Glue them together, front to front.

2. Color four of the 6" plates to look like wheels. Glue the wheels onto the bottom of the pumpkin. Let the glue dry before standing the carriage upright.

3. Cut out a stem using the pattern provided from one 6" plate and color it green. Glue the stem to the top of the pumpkin. (Note: You can cut stems for many pumpkins from one plate.)

Variations

1. Use green construction paper for the stem.

2. Draw doors and windows on the pumpkin.

3. To make the wheels turn, use brass brads to attach the wheels to the pumpkin halves *before* they are glued together.

Literature Selections

Any version of "Cinderella" will do.

Selected Activity

Turn one side of the pumpkin carriage into a clock face. Attach movable hands with a brass brad. When the clock strikes midnight . . . .

United Nations Day

Materials

one 9" paper plate
two 6" paper plates
markers or crayons
scissors
glue

Directions

1. On the back of the 9" plate, write the words *United Nations Day* (or use the cut-out provided on page 15) along the rim. You can color the rest of the plate if you wish.

2. Copy and cut out the continents pattern on page 15. Glue on the bottom of one of the 6" plates. Color the picture.

3. Glue the two 6" plates together, front to front. Glue this, picture side up, to the middle back of the 9" plate.

4. Display on bulletin board.

Selected Activity

This project can be used as part of a geography or social studies curriculum.

Literature Selection

The United Nations 50th Anniversary Book
by Barbara Brenner
Atheneum, 1995

14

Columbus Day

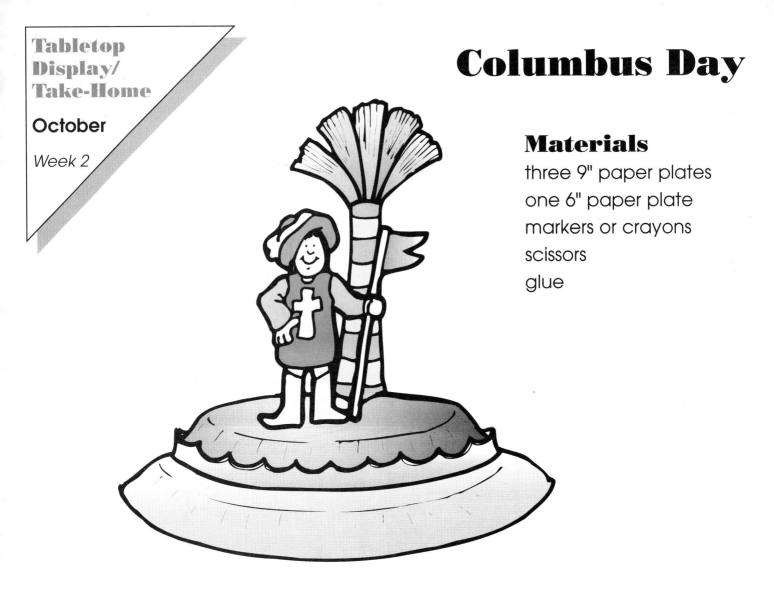

Materials
three 9" paper plates
one 6" paper plate
markers or crayons
scissors
glue

Directions
1. Color the back of one 9" plate blue, this will represent the ocean.
2. Color the back of the 6" plate brown or green to represent land.
3. Stack the land plate on top of the ocean plate and glue in place.
4. From another 9" plate, color and cut out waves. Glue them around the island.
5. From the center of the remaining 9" plate, cut out a tree trunk (pattern on page 17) and color it. Cut out and color palm fronds (pattern on page 17) from the rim of the plate (fringe the edges for leaves). Glue the fronds to the top of the tree. Glue the finished tree to the island.
6. Color and cut out the Columbus reproducible on page 17. Glue him to the island next to the tree.

Literature Selection
My First Columbus Day Book
by Dee Lillegard
Children's Press, 1987

Selected Activity
This project can be used as part of a history curriculum.

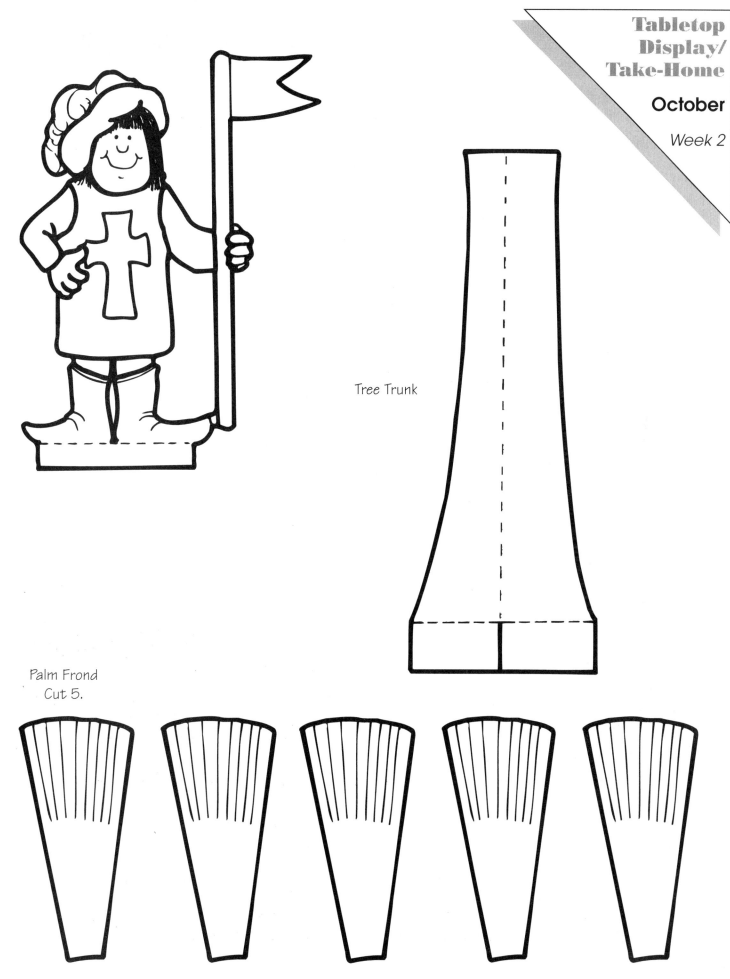

Tree Trunk

Palm Frond
Cut 5.

Birds of a Feather Halloween Mask

Materials

two 9" paper plates
markers or crayons
scissors
glue
yarn

Directions

1. Cut one of the 9" plates in half to create a half-face mask. Mark and cut out eye holes. Color the mask.

2. Use the other half of the plate to cut out feathers. Color and glue the feathers between the eye holes with the feathery edges sticking up and out over the top of the mask.

3. Cut a beak from the second 9" plate and glue it to the bottom of the mask, between the eye holes. (Note: You might be able to get more than one beak out of the plate, which would reduce waste.)

4. Attach yarn to both sides of the mask to tie it in place.

Variation

Use real feathers instead of paper feathers.

Literature Selection

The Best-Ever Costume Party
by Kaffa
Scholastic, 1993

Selected Activity

This project might also be used in a social studies unit featuring costumes and masks of other cultures.

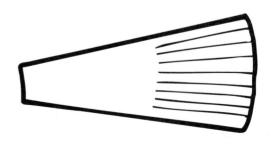

18

My Desk

Materials

three 9" paper plates
markers or crayons
scissors
glue

Directions

1. Color the back of one of the 9" plates. Use your favorite color. Set aside.

2. From another 9" plate, cut a rectangle 5" x 3¹/₂" (13 x 9 cm). On this rectangle write the words *My Desk*. Write your name at the bottom of the rectangle.

3. Cut out a signpost from the pattern on page 20, and glue it to the back of your sign. Fold the tab back at the other end of the post. Put a dot of glue on the tab and glue it to the back of the 9" plate.

4. From the remaining plate, cut a rectangle approximately 5" x 3" (13 x 8 cm). On this rectangle, write the words *Welcome, Parents*.

Variation

For younger children, write out the words *My Desk* and *Welcome, Parents* and copy for the children to cut out and paste in position.

Literature Selection

Starting School
by Janet Ahlberg
Viking, 1988

Selected Activity

Children can write a note to their parents on a 3" x 5" (8 x 13 cm) card and place it under the plate for their parents to find when they visit their child's desk.

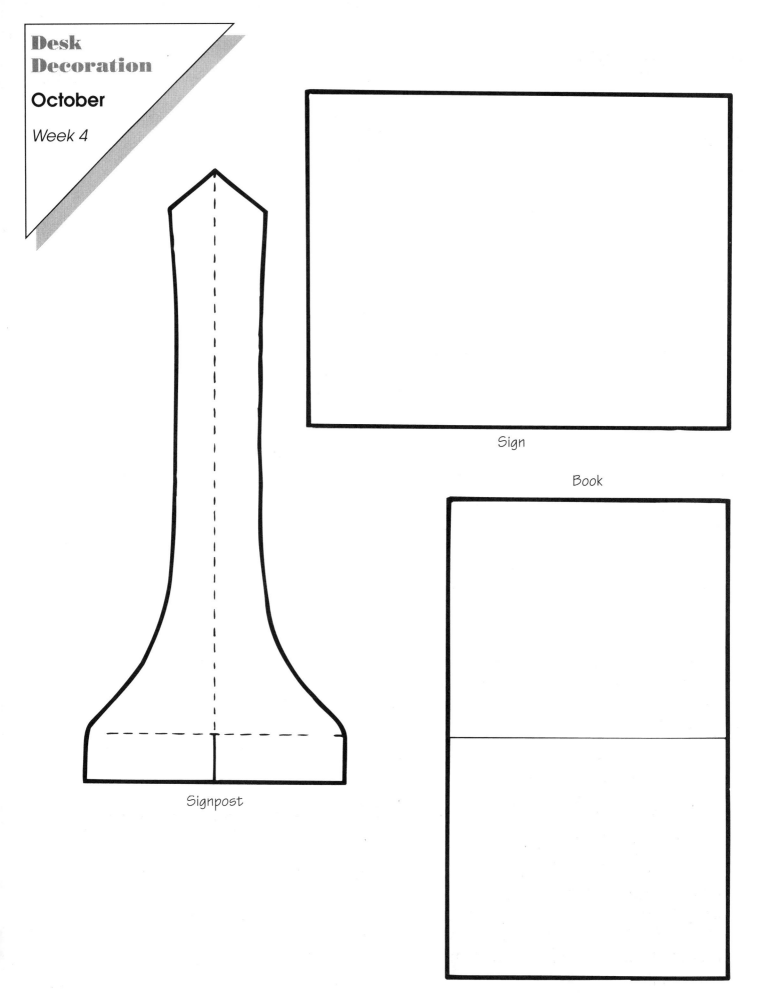

Sign

Book

Signpost

Going South

Materials

two 9" paper plates
two 6" paper plates
yarn
markers and crayons
scissors
glue

Directions

1. From the center of both 9" plates, cut out two large clouds (pattern on page 22). When cutting them out, lay one plate on top of the other so that the clouds will be identical. Repeat this step with the 6" plates.

2. From the scraps, cut out and color four birds, using the pattern on page 22.

3. Cut five pieces of yarn in the following lengths:

   9" (23 cm), 12" (30 cm), 14" (36 cm), 18" (46 cm), 20" (51 cm)

4. Glue one end of the 14" (36 cm) piece of yarn to the top of one of the 9" plate clouds. Glue one end of each of the remaining lengths of yarn to the bottom of the same cloud. Glue the matching 9" cloud on top to hold the yarn in place.

5. Glue one of the smaller clouds onto the 14" (36 cm) piece of yarn approximately 2" (5 cm) above the large cloud. Glue the other small cloud on top, with the yarn running between them.

6. Glue the birds to the bottom of the remaining pieces of yarn to complete your mobile.

Variation

Hang raindrops, snowflakes, airplanes or hot air balloons from the clouds.

Literature Selections

The Great Ball Game
by Joseph Bruchac
Dial, 1994

A Year of Birds
by Ashley Wolff
Puffin, 1984

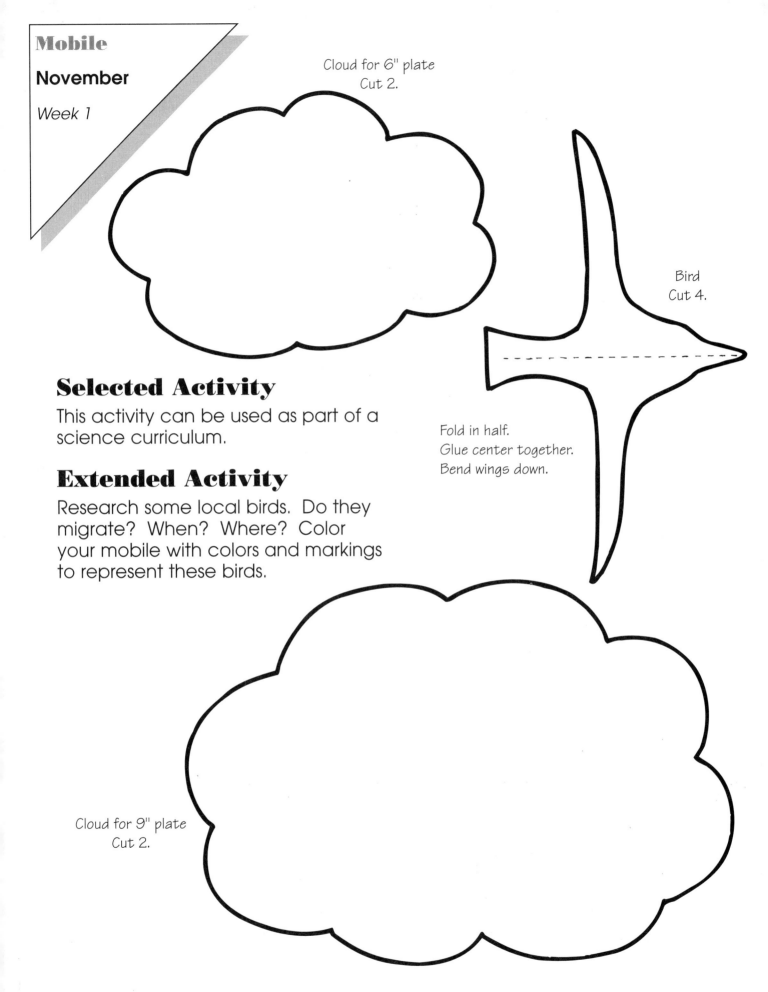

Cloud for 6" plate
Cut 2.

Bird
Cut 4.

Selected Activity

This activity can be used as part of a science curriculum.

Extended Activity

Research some local birds. Do they migrate? When? Where? Color your mobile with colors and markings to represent these birds.

Fold in half.
Glue center together.
Bend wings down.

Cloud for 9" plate
Cut 2.

Fall Mouse

Materials

four 9" paper plates
markers or crayons
scissors
glue

Directions

1. Color the middle of the back of a 9" paper plate blue and then color the rim brown or dark green. This will be the base plate.

2. Using the pattern on page 24, cut out a large maple leaf from one of the 9" paper plates for the boat. Color in fall colors.

3. Use another 9" paper plate to cut out 12 small maple leaves (see pattern on page 24) for the decoration around the edge of the base plate. Color these leaves in a variety of fall colors.

4. Copy the mouse on page 24, color it and glue it to the center of the remaining 9" plate. Cut it out around the outline.

5. Glue the edging leaves around the rim of the base plate. Glue the back middle of the boat leaf to the blue middle of the base plate. Curl up the edges of the boat leaf. Glue the mouse into the boat as shown.

Variations

1. Have the mouse hold a toothpick or sliver of paper for an oar.

2. Write the words *Over the river and through the woods . . .* around the base plate where the blue meets the colored rim.

Literature Selections

A Book of Seasons
by Alice and Martin Provensen
Random House, 1976

Also by the same authors:
The Seasons at Maple Hill Farm

Frederick
by Leo Lionni
Pantheon, 1967

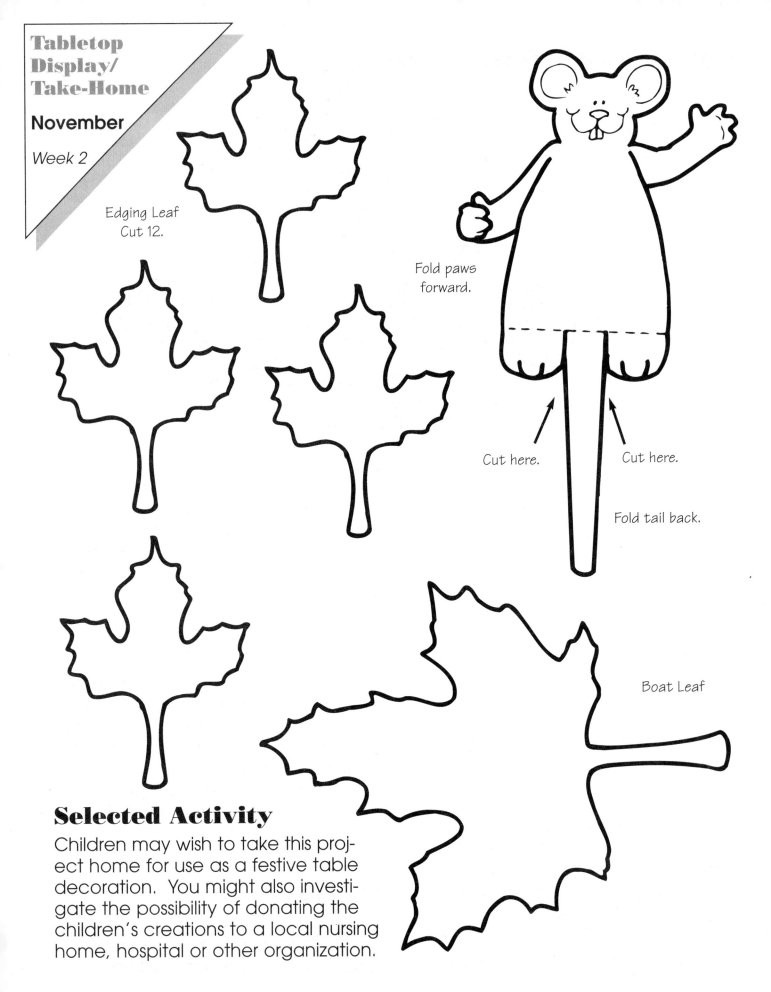

Edging Leaf
Cut 12.

Fold paws forward.

Cut here.   Cut here.

Fold tail back.

Boat Leaf

Selected Activity

Children may wish to take this project home for use as a festive table decoration. You might also investigate the possibility of donating the children's creations to a local nursing home, hospital or other organization.

Thanksgiving Turkey

Materials

five 9" paper plates
five 6" paper plates
markers or crayons
scissors
glue

Directions

1. Color the back of a 9" and 6" paper plate green. Cut a 3¹/₂" (9 cm) long slit in the middle of the 6" plate. Glue the 6" plate to the 9" plate, front to back.

2. Color the backs of two 9" plates brown. Glue them together front to front. This will be the turkey's body. Color the backs of two 6" plates orange and glue them together front to front. This will be the turkey's face. Glue the two 6" plates to the middle of the 9" plates.

3. Color the back and front of a 6" plate brown, cut it in half and fringe the ends to look like feathers (wing pattern on page 27). Glue the wings to the brown body of the turkey.

4. Cut out and color (use orange, yellow and red) the tail feathers (pattern on page 27) and glue them to the back of the top of the turkey body. Cut out eyes, two beaks and a wattle (patterns on pages 26 and 27). Color the beak yellow. Color the wattle red. Glue these pieces to the orange turkey face.

5. Put glue into the slit on the green plate and set the bottom of the turkey body into the slit. Hold the turkey in place for a few seconds while the glue dries. Cut out and color some turkey feet (pattern on page 27) and glue them to the green plate in front of the body.

Variation

Copy the turkey eyes, beak, wattle and feet onto construction paper and precut for smaller children.

25

Literature Selection

'Twas the Night Before Thanksgiving
by Dave Pilkey
Orchard Books, 1994

Selected Activity

Children may wish to take this project home for use as a festive table decoration. You might also investigate the possibility of donating the children's creations to a local nursing home, hospital or other organization.

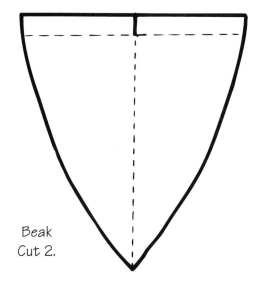

Beak
Cut 2.

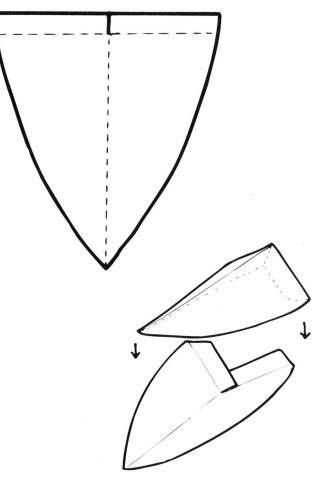

Eyes

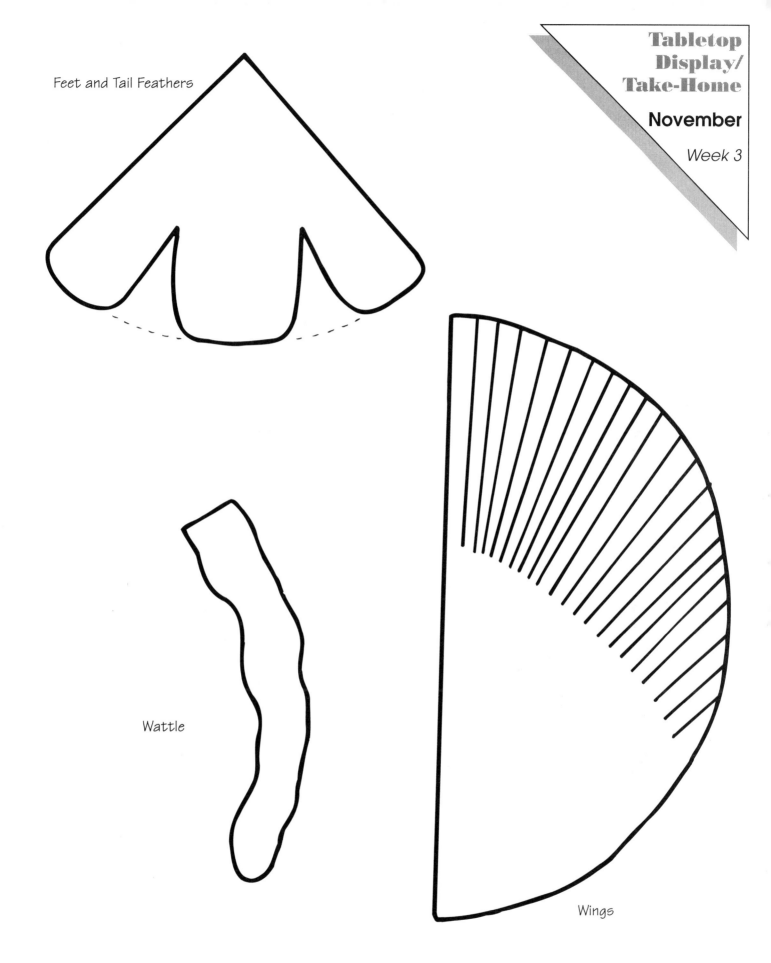

Feet and Tail Feathers

Wattle

Wings

Touchdown Game

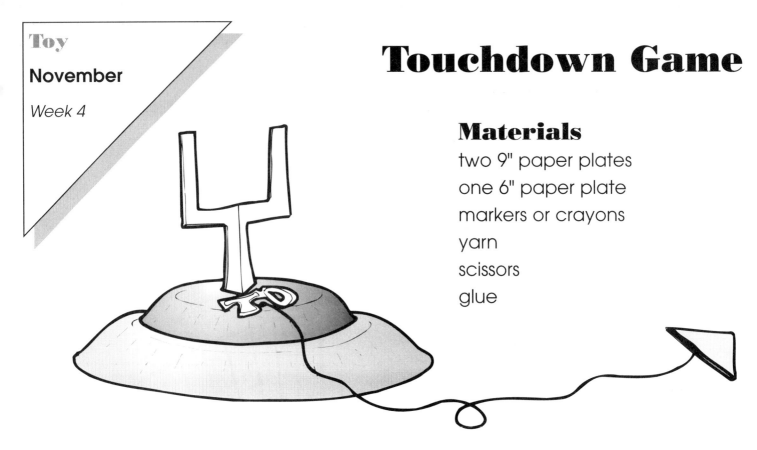

Materials

two 9" paper plates
one 6" paper plate
markers or crayons
yarn
scissors
glue

Directions

1. Color the back of one of the 9" paper plates green.

2. Color the back of the 6" plate brown. Center the front of the 6" plate on the back of the 9" plate and glue in place.

3. Cut a goalpost from the other 9" plate (pattern on page 29). Put a dot of glue on the tab and glue the goalpost to the top of the 6" plate.

4. Glue one end of a 2' (.6 m) long piece of yarn to the 6" plate, directly in front of the goalpost. Cut out the letters *T* and *D* (patterns on page 29). Color the letters and glue onto the 6" plate, covering the top of the yarn.

5. Make a small triangle out of scraps from the 9" plate. See the guidelines for making the football on page 29. Glue the end of the yarn in the center of the triangle. Fold the ends of the triangle over the yarn end and glue shut.

6. Place the game on a level surface. Hold the triangle up on one end about a foot away from the goalpost. Snap it through the uprights with your fingers.

Literature Selection

Kick Pass and Run
by Leonard Kessler
HarperCollins, 1966

Selected Activity

Use this project to kick off an investigation of ball games in other cultures or at other times in history. Do your students know the Pilgrims and Indians played ball games at the first Thanksgiving? The ball was made of leather and stuffed with feathers.

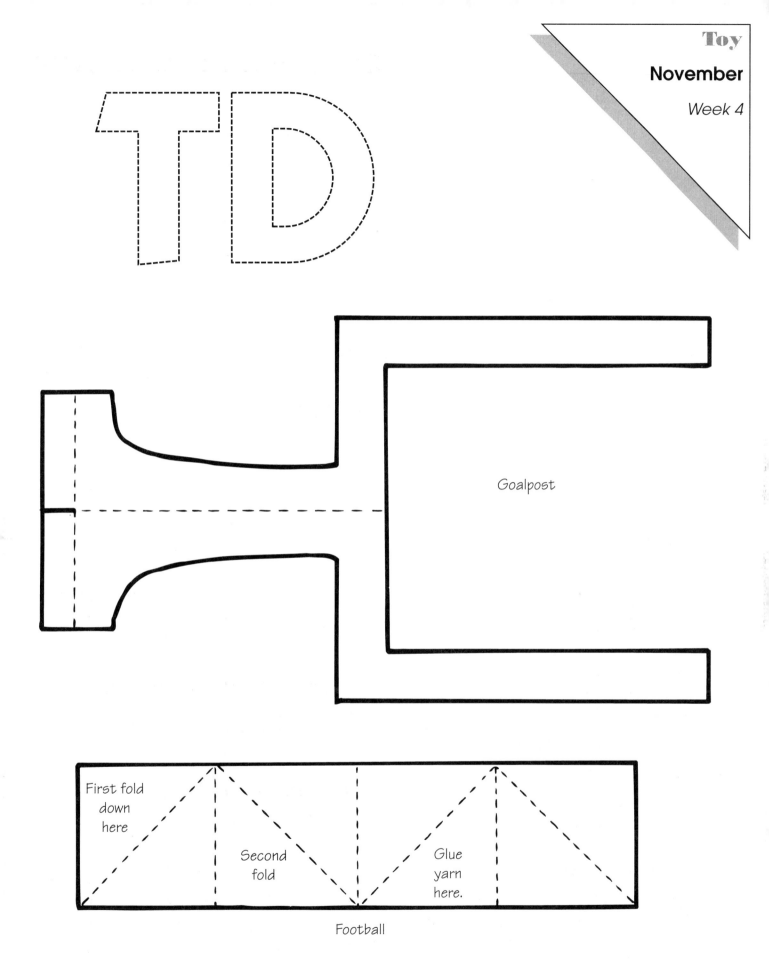

Goalpost

First fold
down
here

Second
fold

Glue
yarn
here.

Football

Holiday Cardholder

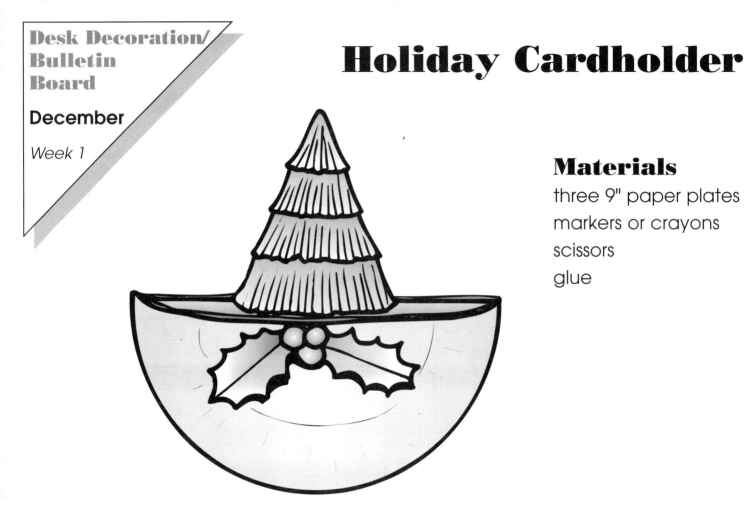

Materials

three 9" paper plates
markers or crayons
scissors
glue

Directions

1. Cut one of the 9" plates in half. Color the back of this half red or green.
2. Cut a second plate in half, but this time cut a tall triangle up from the middle to a point on the rim. This will represent a Christmas tree*. Color the tree on the front of this plate. Cut fringed paper branches from the scraps, color and glue onto the tree.
3. Glue the first colored half to the bottom of the tree half, front to front, to form a pouch.

Variations

*This project can be used as a holder for any holiday by changing the tree cut-out to: a Star of David for Hanukkah, a bunny or chick for Easter, a turkey for Thanksgiving, seven candles for Kwanzaa, a birthday cake for a classroom birthday, a heart for Valentine's Day, etc. See patterns on pages 31 and 32.

Literature Selection

Choose a story appropriate for the holiday.

Selected Activity

Have children create original cards to place in the holder. You can recycle old greeting cards by pasting white paper over the verse and letting children come up with their own messages.

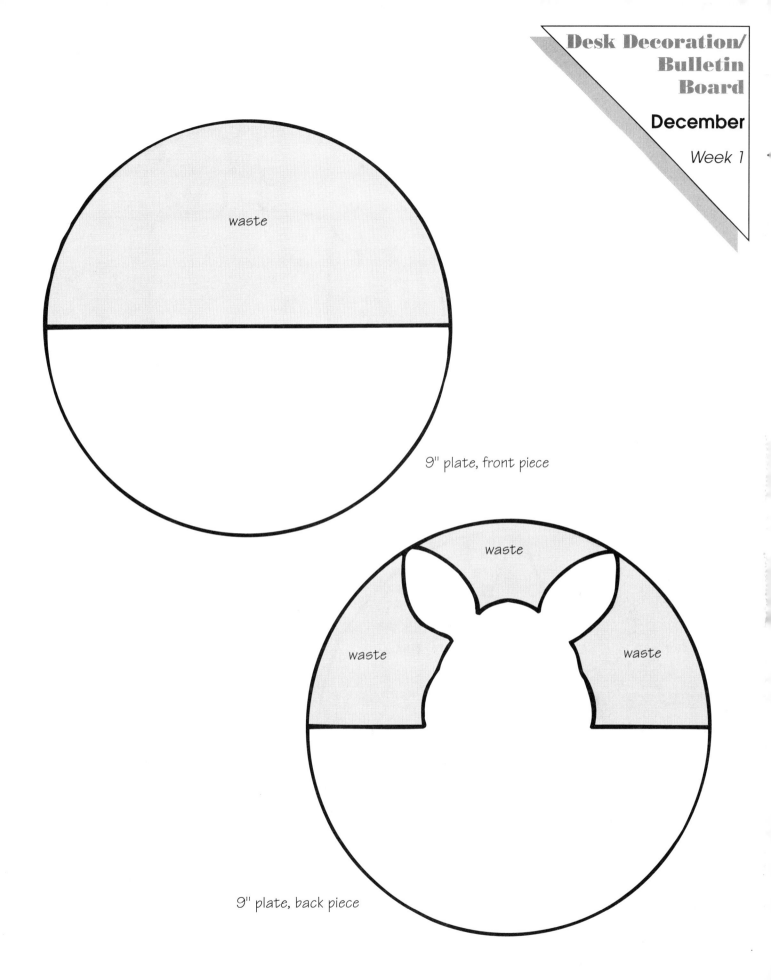

waste

9" plate, front piece

waste

waste

waste

9" plate, back piece

Sample Variation Patterns

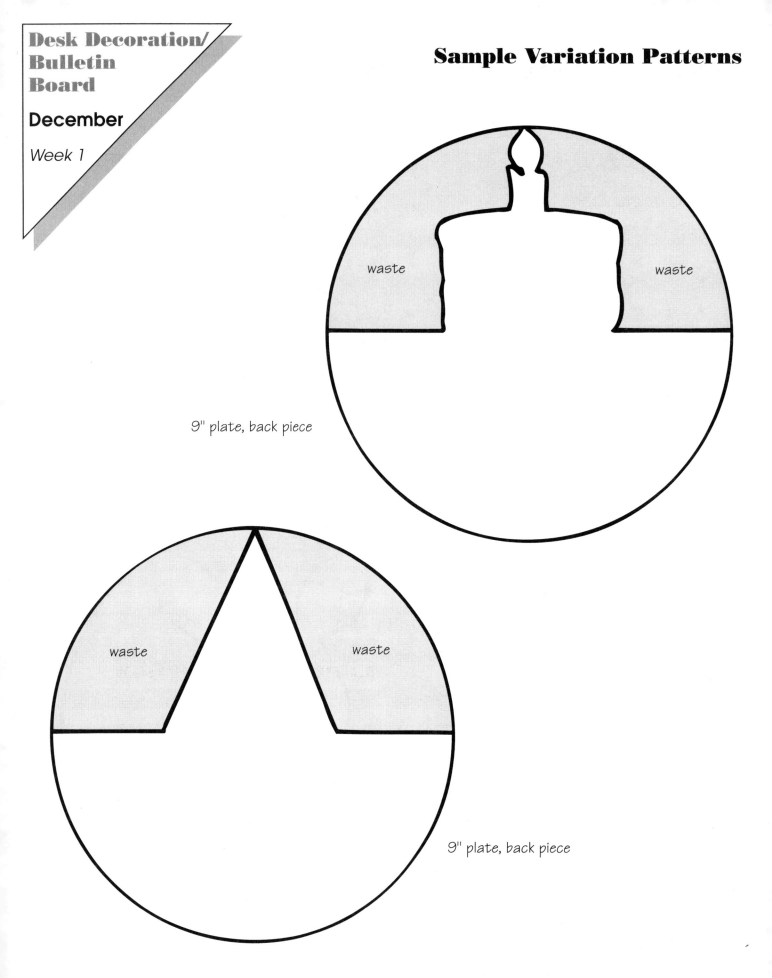

9" plate, back piece

waste   waste

waste   waste

9" plate, back piece

Oh, Christmas Tree!

Materials

two 6" paper plates
markers or crayons
scissors
glue

Directions

1. Cut four branches (patterns on page 34) as wide as the rims of the plates in these lengths:

   $1^1/2$" (4 cm), $2^1/2$" (6 cm), $3^1/2$" (9 cm) and $4^1/2$" (11 cm).

   Color the branches green and color on decorations.

2. From the scraps, cut out a tree pot, a star and two strips $5^1/2$" (14 cm) long and $^1/2$" (1.25 cm) wide (patterns on page 34). Glue the strips together to form the tree trunk. Color the trunk brown, the pot red and the star yellow.

3. Glue the branches to the tree trunk, graduating size from top (shortest) to bottom (longest). Glue the star to the top. Glue the bottom of the trunk to the back of the pot.

Variations

1. Use glitter to make the star sparkle.

2. Cut out construction paper ornaments and glue them on.

Literature Selection

Christmas Tree Farm
by Sandra Jordan
Orchard Books, 1993

Selected Activity

Use these trees to create an attractive bulletin board display. Use a dark color for the background and cotton batting for snow.

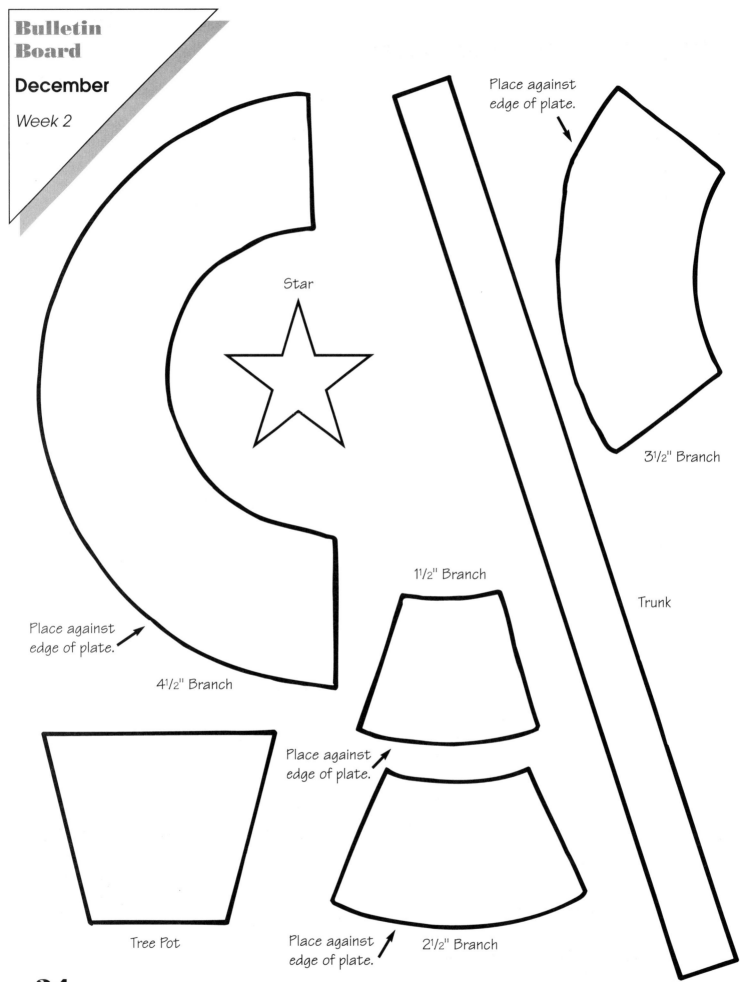

Star

Place against edge of plate.

3 1/2" Branch

Place against edge of plate.

1 1/2" Branch

Trunk

4 1/2" Branch

Place against edge of plate.

Tree Pot

Place against edge of plate.

2 1/2" Branch

34

Hanukkah Candle

Materials

one 6" paper plate
two 9" paper plates
markers or crayons
scissors
glue

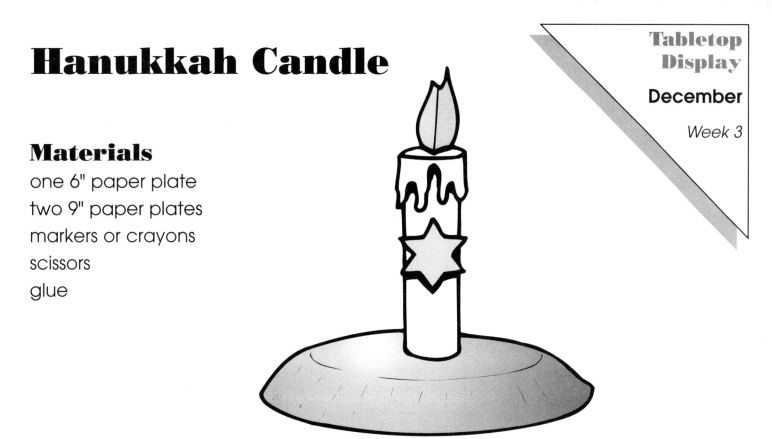

Directions

1. Color the back of the 6" plate purple. Set aside.

2. From one of the 9" plates, cut out a rectangle 4$^1/_2$" (11 cm) wide by 5" (13 cm) long. Roll it into a tube and glue the edge to make a candlestick. Glue one end of the candle to the middle of the purple plate.

3. From the remaining 9" plate, cut out a Star of David and a candle flame (patterns on page 36). Color them yellow. Glue the Star of David to the front of the candlestick, about halfway up.

4. Cut out a top for the candle that looks like dripping wax (pattern on page 36). Glue it to the top of the candlestick to form a cap. Bend the bottom of the flame to form a tab and glue the flame to the middle of the candle cap.

Variations

1. Have your students make enough candles to form a menorah.

2. A small gift or message can be inserted inside the candlestick before gluing on the cap.

Literature Selections

My First Hanukkah Book
by Aileen Fisher
Children's Press, 1985

The Story of Hanukkah
by Amy Erlich
Dial, 1989

Selected Activity

This project can be used as part of a social studies curriculum. Ask your students to research other Hanukkah traditions and share the information with the class.

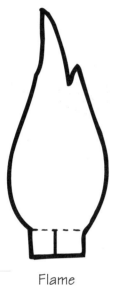

Flame

Candle
Roll into a tube.

Star of David

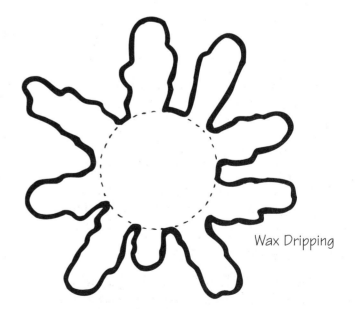

Wax Dripping

Fold down on dotted lines.
Glue flame to top.

Kwanzaa

Materials

four 9" paper plates
markers or crayons
scissors
glue

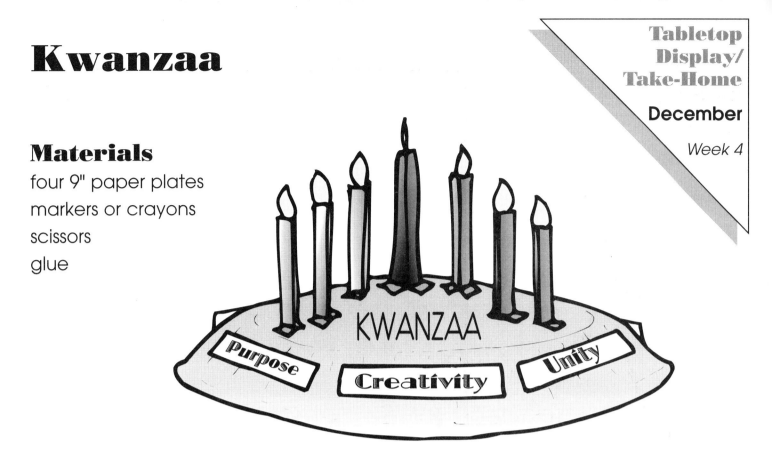

Directions

1. Color the back of a 9" plate yellow. Write the word *KWANZAA* in the center.

2. Use another 9" plate to cut out seven 3" x 1" (7 x 2.5 cm) rectangles (pattern on page 38). These will be the candles. Color three of them red, three green and one black. Fold each rectangle in half the long way. Cut a small (about 1/2" (1.25 cm)) slit in the bottom of each one to make tabs. Bend the tabs out. Place a small dot of glue at the top of each rectangle and pinch shut. Place dots of glue on the bottom of each tab. Glue the candle tabs to the yellow plate in a semicircle around the inner rim.

3. Cut out and color seven flames (pattern on page 38) for the candles and glue them to the tops of the candlesticks.

4. On the remaining plates, write the seven principles of Kwanzaa (or use patterns provided on page 38), cut them out and glue them around the rim of the 9" plate.

Literature Selections

It's Kwanzaa Time
by Linda and Clay Goss
Philomel, 1994

My First Kwanzaa Book
by Deborah M. Chocolate
Scholastic, 1992

Seven Candles for Kwanzaa
by Andrea D. Pinkney
Dial, 1993

Selected Activity

This activity may be used as part of a social studies curriculum. Have children investigate the Kwanzaa celebration. What is its history? What are some of the other elements of the celebration?

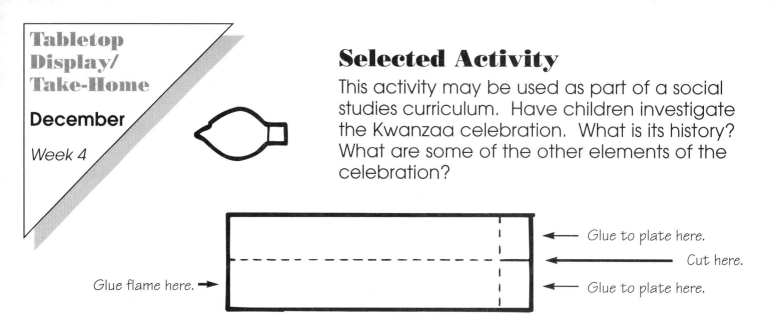

Glue to plate here.

Cut here.

Glue flame here. ➤

Glue to plate here.

Cooperative Economics

Self-Determination

Creativity   Purpose

Collective Work

Faith   Unity

Happy New Year's Hat

Materials

four 9" paper plates
one 6" paper plate
markers or crayons
scissors
glue
yarn

Directions

1. Cut the middle from one 9" plate, leave the rim intact. Color the back of the rim. Color the back of another 9" plate and glue the rim to it, front to back.

2. Color the back of the 6" plate and glue it, front down, onto the solid-colored 9" plate.

3. Color the back of the third 9" plate. Cut it in half. Glue the rims together, front to front, leaving the cut edge open.

4. From the remaining 9" plate, color and cut feathers and glue them to the top of the hat.

5. Attach a 12" (30 cm) piece of yarn to either side so children can tie on their hats.

39

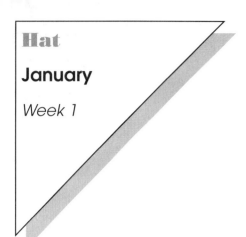

Variation

Instead of feathers for the top of their hats, children can cut out other objects or free-form designs.

Literature Selections

Goodbye Old Year, Hello New Year
by Frank Modell
Greenwillow, 1984

Happy New Year
by Emily Kellogg
Carolrhoda Books, 1984

Un-Happy New Year, Emma!
by James Stevenson
Greenwillow, 1989

Selected Activity

This project can also be used for Hat Day on January 20th.

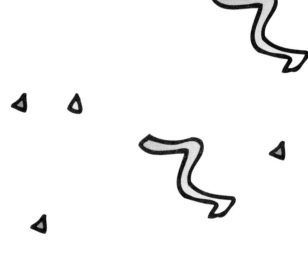

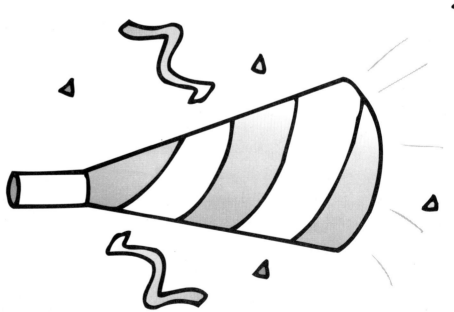

I Have a Dream, Too . . .

Materials

one 9" paper plate
one 6" paper plate
markers or crayons
scissors
glue

I have a dream, too . . .

Directions

1. Cut a cloud from the center of the 9" plate using the pattern on page 42. At the top of the cloud, write the words *I have a dream, too . . .* Ask your students to draw or write about their dream in the space on the plate underneath the words.

2. From the scraps of the 9" plate, cut out the nose (pattern on page 42). Bend a $1/8$" (.3 cm) tab at the base and glue the tab to the middle of the 6" plate. Draw on eyes and a mouth.

3. Glue the cloud to the top of the face so that it looks like a thought.

Variations

1. Have each student draw her own face on the 6" plate.

2. Use scraps from the 9" plate to fashion hair, ears, bow tie, etc., for the 6" plate face.

Literature Selection

Martin Luther King Day
by Janet McDonnell
Children's Press, 1993

Selected Activities

This project can be used as part of a social studies or history curriculum. Ask your students to focus their dreams on a specific issue (ie. world peace, hunger, the homeless, etc.).

Create a bulletin board with the students' work. A rainbow or multicolored background would make an effective display.

Cloud

Nose

Nose

Face

Chinese New Year Dragon

Materials
two 6" paper plates
two 9" paper plates
markers or crayons
scissors
glue
pen/pencil

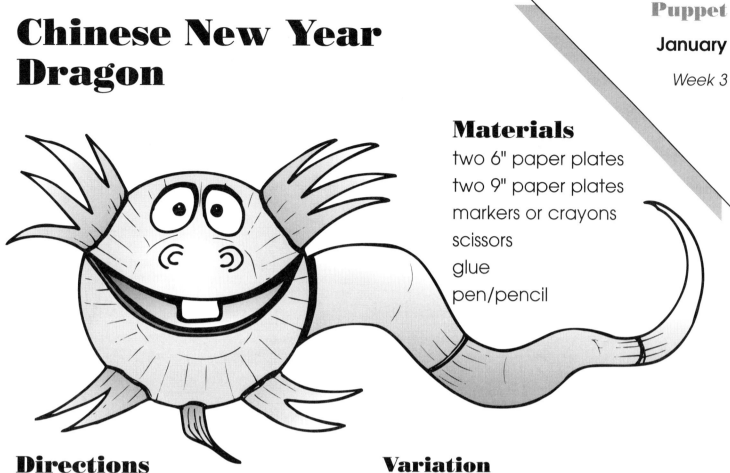

Directions

1. Color the back of a 6" plate with green, red and yellow. Cut out a smile as wide as the plate. Glue this plate front to front with the second 6" plate.

2. Cut a tooth and eyes (patterns on page 44) from one of the 9" plates. Draw on nostrils. Glue the tooth and eyes into place.

3. Cut a wavy tail out the remaining 9" plate. Cut it in three sections. (Make the sections graduate in size from wide to just a point.) Glue the tail sections together. Color the tail. Make a tab at the wide end by folding it back ¹/2" (1.25 cm). Glue the tail to the back of the head.

4. From the scraps, cut out and color the "fins" (patterns on page 44) and glue them in place.

Variation
Glue a craft stick to the back of the head. Wave it in the air and watch the tail dance!

Literature Selection
Chin Chiang and the Dragon's Dance by Ian Wallace
Margaret K. McElderry Books, 1984

Selected Activity
Use this activity as part of a social studies curriculum. Have children investigate the Chinese New Year celebration. What does the dragon represent? What else can they find out about the symbols and traditions of this ancient holiday?

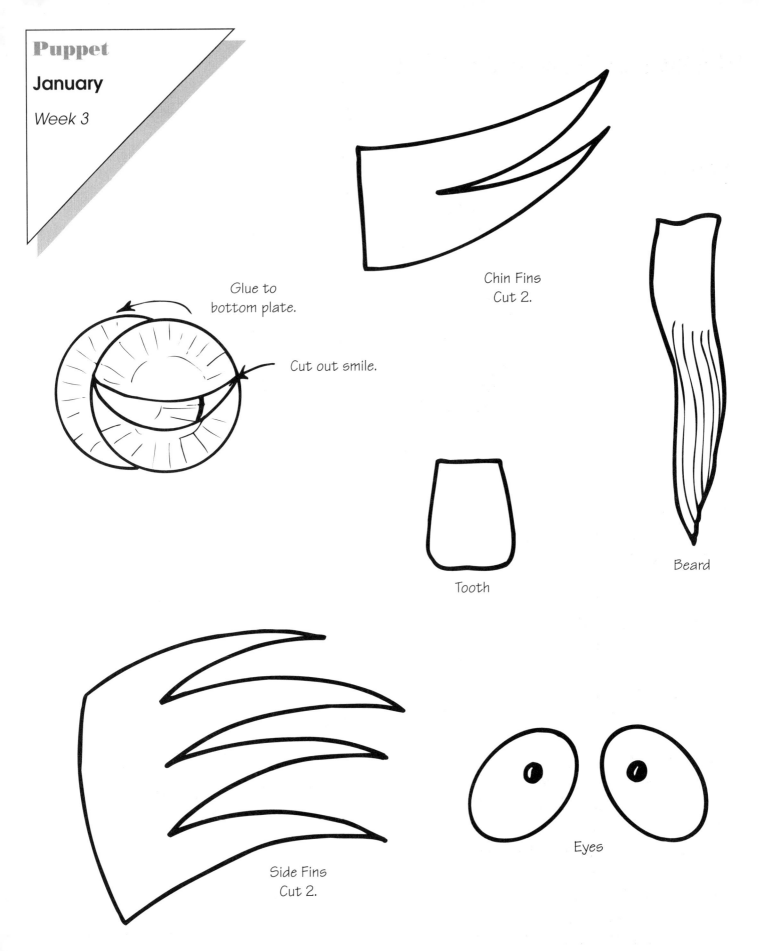

Chin Fins
Cut 2.

Glue to
bottom plate.

Cut out smile.

Beard

Tooth

Side Fins
Cut 2.

Eyes

Winter Snowflake

Materials

four 6" paper plates
two 9" paper plates
yarn
scissors
glue

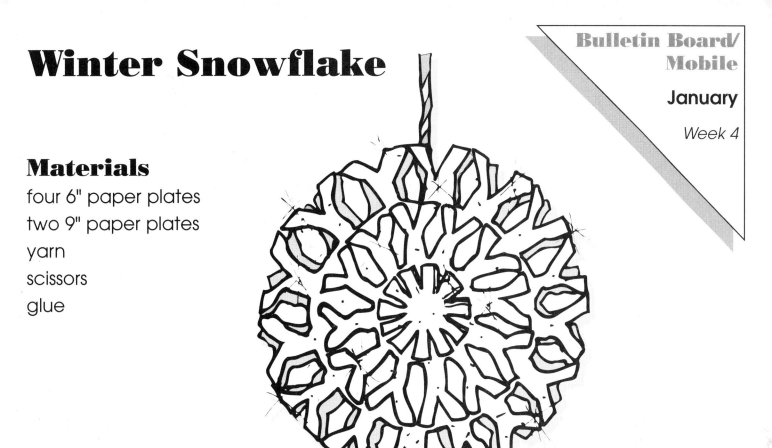

Directions

1. Make cut-outs all around the rim of one of the 9" plates so that it resembles the edges of a snow-flake. See patterns on page 46. Do this to two of the 6" plates as well. Set aside.

2. Cut large circles from the middle of the remaining 6" plates. Cut the rims as you did on the other plates.

3. Glue the end of a 2' (.6 m) piece of yarn to the middle back of one of the 9" plates. Glue the 9" plates together, back to back.

4. Glue the 6" plates in the middle on either side of the 9" plates. Now glue the smaller circles in the middle on either side of the 6" plates. Let the glue dry before you hang it up.

Variation

You can use glue and glitter to dec-orate the snowflake.

Literature Selection

When Will It Snow?
by Syd Hoff
Harper & Row, 1971

Selected Activity

Hang the snowflakes from the ceiling for an attractive display. You can also eliminate the yarn and pin the snowflakes to a bulletin board. Students might wish to write their names on their snowflakes using glitter glue or a silver marker.

Extended Activity

Use this activity as part of a science curriculum. Look for references on growing crystals.

45

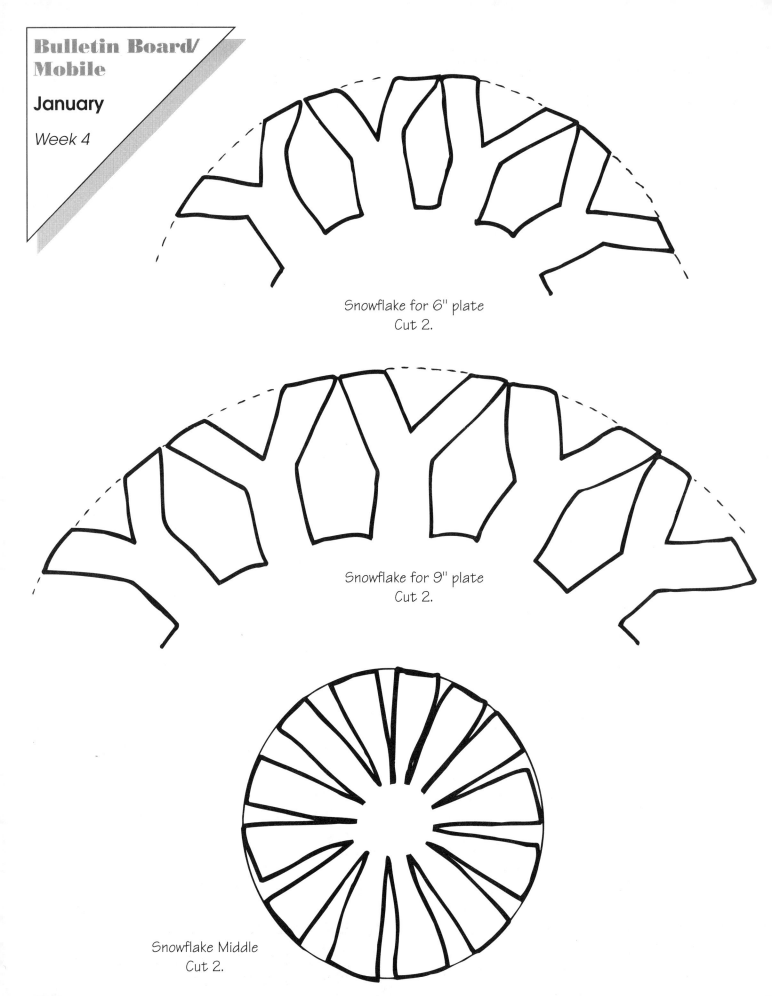

Snowflake for 6" plate
Cut 2.

Snowflake for 9" plate
Cut 2.

Snowflake Middle
Cut 2.

Gobbler's Knob Groundhog Day

Materials

four 9" paper plates
yarn
markers or crayons
scissors
glue

Directions

1. Color the back of one plate to look like grass. Cut a 3" x ¹/2" (8 x 1.25 cm) hole in the middle of the plate. Add a little brown color around the hole. Write *Gobbler's Knob* around the rim of the plate or use the cut-out on page 48.

2. Glue the plate to a second 9" plate, front to front.

3. Cut out and color a short signpost and a 1¹/2" x 1¹/2" (4 x 4 cm) sign. Write *Phil is asleep!* on the sign and glue it to the signpost. See patterns on page 49. Bend up the bottom of the signpost about ¹/2" (1.25 cm) to make a tab. Glue the tab to the grass.

4. Copy the picture of Phil (pattern on page 48). Color and glue it to the third 9" plate. Cut out the figure including the rectangle at the base. Glue one end of a 7" (18 cm) piece of yarn to the back of Phil. Slightly roll in the edges of the rectangle and slide it into the hole, facedown.

5. Cut a large circle out of the last plate. Cut the circle in half. On one half glue the words *Welcome to Punxsutawney, PA* (pattern on page 49). Glue this half to the other half with the free end of the piece of yarn in between.

6. Pull Phil out of his hole to see (or not see) his shadow!

Literature Selections

It's Groundhog Day
by Steven Kroll
Holiday House, 1987

Will Spring Ever Come to Gobbler's Knob?
by Julia S. Montran
Literary Publications, 1992

Selected Activity

Add a a flashlight to this activity and create real shadows!

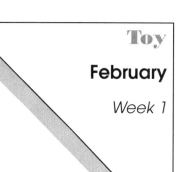

Phil is asleep!

Welcome to Punxsutawney, PA

Heart Chain

Materials

four 6" paper plates
pink or red yarn
scissors
glue

Directions

1. Cut a heart out of the middle of the four plates, leaving the rims intact (pattern on page 51).
2. Cut a piece of yarn 2' (.6 cm) long. About 4" (10 cm) from one end, glue two of the rims, front to front, with the yarn through the middle.
3. Next, glue two of the cut-out hearts under the rims. Again, sandwiching the yarn. Repeat steps 2 and 3 with the remaining rims and heart.

Variations

1. Color the plates and hearts or add glitter, lace, stickers, etc.
2. Write children's names or *Be My Valentine* on the cut-out hearts. See other ideas on page 51.

Literature Selection

Valentine Foxes
by Clyde Watson
Orchard Books, 1992

Selected Activity

Hang the heart chains from the ceiling for an attractive mobile.

Write a question on the front of the cut-out heart and the answer on the back. Use either way–children looking at the question would have to give the correct answer or children looking at the answer would have to pose the correct question.

50

Plates will be front to front.

6" plate faceup

Glue together.

6" plate facedown

Love

Happy
Hearts!

Happy
Valentine's
Day!

Presidential Silhouettes

Materials

three 9" paper plates
markers or crayons
scissors
glue

Directions

1. Color the front of one of the 9" plates in red and blue stripes.

2. From the remaining two plates, cut out seven stars, *VOTE* and a wavy banner (patterns on pages 53 and 54).

3. Copy and cut out the presidential silhouette you want to use (patterns on page 54). Write the name of the President on the banner. Color the banner yellow.

4. Glue the banner across the lower half of the striped plate. Glue the stars around the rim of the striped plate. Glue the silhouette in the center of the plate.

Variations

1. Add glitter to the stars.

2. Use a newspaper or magazine picture instead of the silhouette.

Literature Selection

President's Day
by Laura Alden
Children's Press, 1994

Selected Activities

Use this activity in your social studies curriculum.

Use this project to make a festive border for your bulletin board.

Extended Activity

A lamp, a sheet and a clothesline can turn into a lesson on shadows and silhouettes. Students will have fun parading behind the sheet and seeing if their classmates can guess who they are!

52

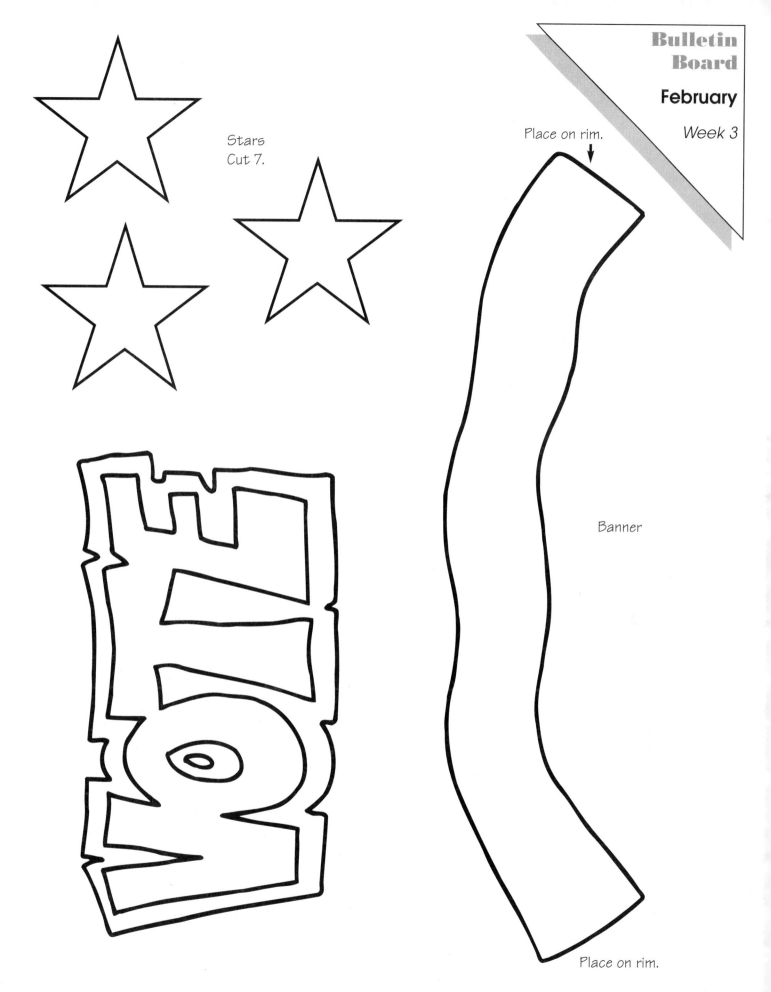

Stars
Cut 7.

Place on rim.

Banner

Place on rim.

Lincoln Silhouette

Washington Silhouette

Let's Go Skiing

Materials

two 6" paper plates
one 9" paper plate or white paper
cotton
markers or crayons
scissors
glue

Directions

1. Copy the skier (pattern on page 56) for each student. Glue it onto the middle of the 9" plate or piece of white paper. Color the skier and cut it out. Bend at the ankles to make feet. Set aside.

2. From one of the 6" plates, cut out and color 5" (13 cm) skis (pattern on page 56). Set aside.

3. Glue the skier's feet to the skis. Glue the skis to the bottom front of the second 6" plate. Glue cotton to the plate for snow.

Variation

1. Add paper strips for ski poles.

2. Cut a hat, scarf and mittens out of felt or colored construction paper to dress your skier.

Literature Selection

A Very Young Skier
by Jill Krementz
Puffin, 1992

Selected Activity

Use this project in your health curriculum to discuss fitness or lifetime sports.

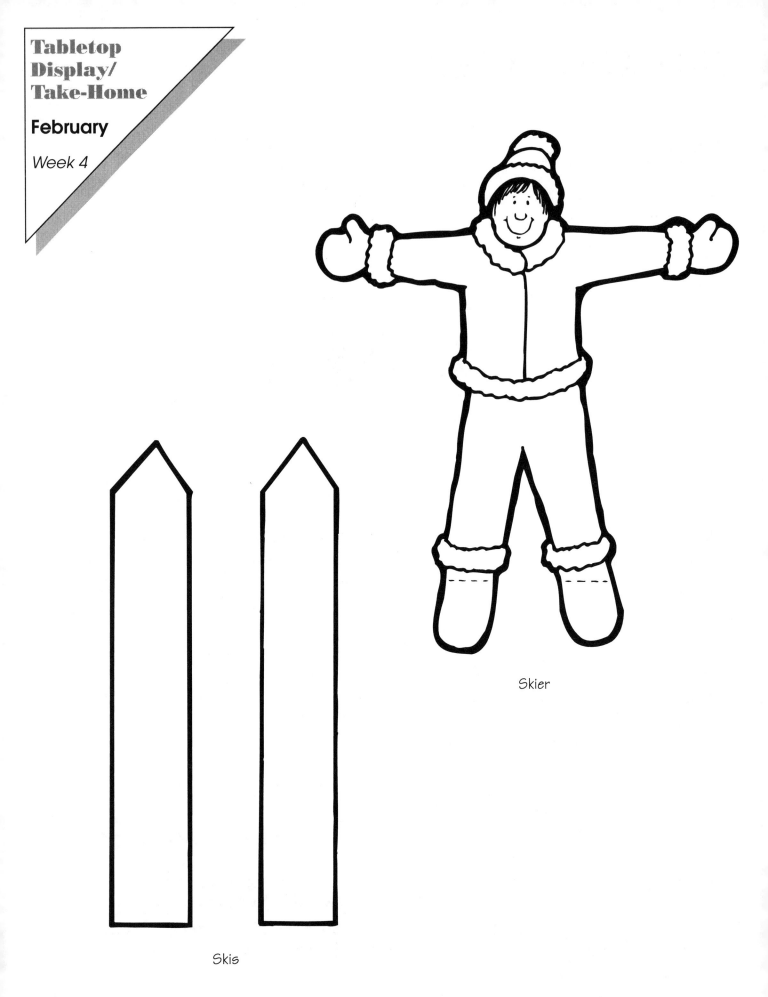

Skier

Skis

This Little Piggy

Materials

one 9" paper plate
four 6" paper plates
markers or crayons
scissors
glue

Directions

1. Use a pink marker or crayon to color the back of the 9" plate.

2. Color the back of one of the 6" plates pink and draw on nostrils and a mouth. Glue this snout to the bottom half of the colored side of the 9" plate. See patterns on page 58.

3. Cut large circles from the centers of two of the 6" plates. Draw on eyes. Glue the eyes to the 9" plate directly above the snout.

4. Cut the remaining 6" plate in half. Cut one of the halves in half again for ears. Color and glue to the back of the 9" plate so that the ears stick out over the top. Curl down, slightly.

Variation

You can make this into a mask by cutting out eye holes and attaching yarn ear loops to either side.

Literature Selections

The Piggy in the Puddle
by Charlotte Pomerantz
Macmillan, 1974

Zeke Pippin
by William Steig
HarperCollins, 1993

Any version of "The Three Little Pigs."

Selected Activity

Enliven your creative dramatics curriculum by using these masks for a performance of "The Three Little Pigs."

57

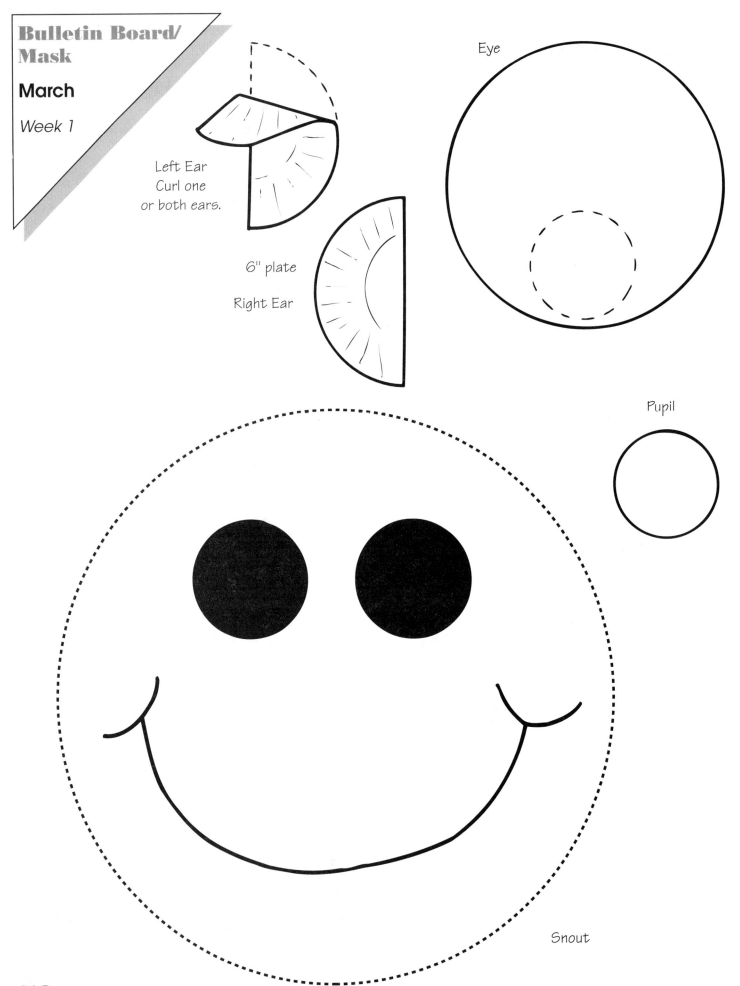

Eye

Left Ear
Curl one
or both ears.

6" plate

Right Ear

Pupil

Snout

Leprechaun Toadstool: St. Patrick's Day

Materials

three 9" paper plates
one 6" paper plate
markers or crayons
scissors
glue

Directions

1. Color the back of the 6" plate green.

2. Cut away 1/8 of one of the 9" plates. Color the back and roll it into a toadstool stem with the flat bottom larger than the top. Glue the flat bottom to the green 6" plate. See guidelines on page 60.

3. Cut a 3" (8 cm) "V" into the second 9" plate. Color the back, overlap the cut sides and glue them together. This forms the top of the toadstool. Glue the top to the stem.

4. Cut out and color a door and a four-leaf clover (patterns on page 60) from the remaining 9" plate. Glue them into place.

Variation

Make a little leprechaun to stand by the door of the toadstool. Page 61 has flower patterns you can use to decorate your toadstool.

Literature Selections

St. Patrick's Day
by Gail Gibbons
Holiday House, 1994

St. Patrick's Day in the Morning
by Eve Bunting
Clarion, 1990

Selected Activity

By eliminating the St. Patrick's Day theme, this project can be used in a science curriculum.

59

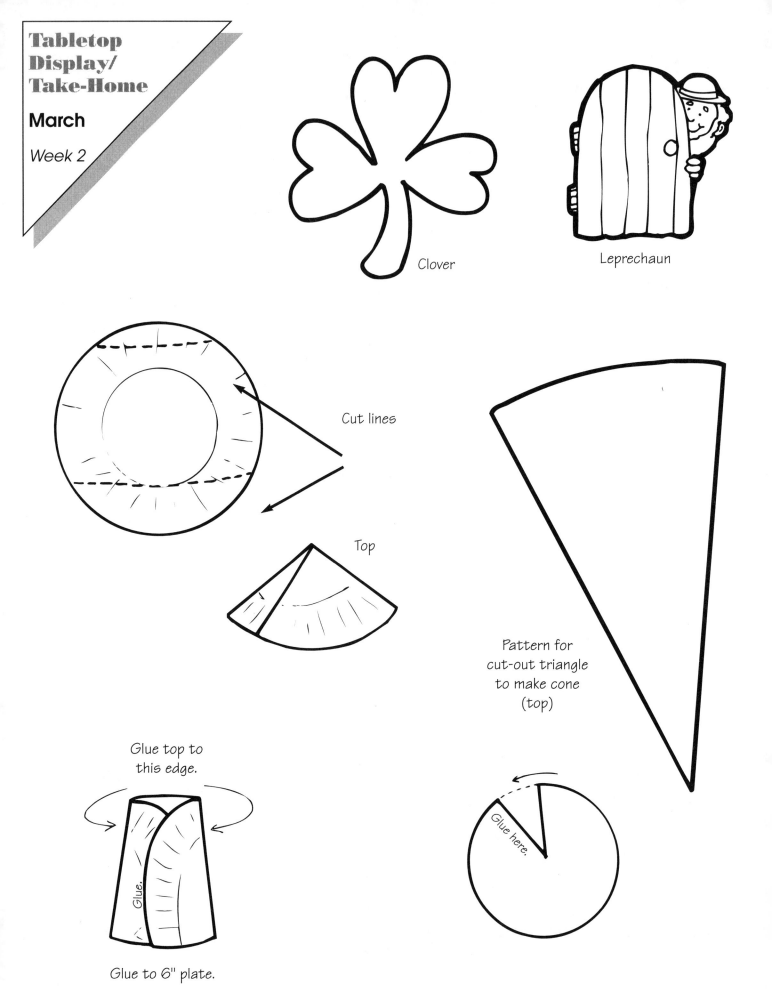

Clover

Leprechaun

Cut lines

Top

Pattern for cut-out triangle to make cone (top)

Glue top to this edge.

Glue.

Glue here.

Glue to 6" plate.

Flower

Flower

Flower

Leaves

Leaf

Flower

Leaf

Soaring Swallow

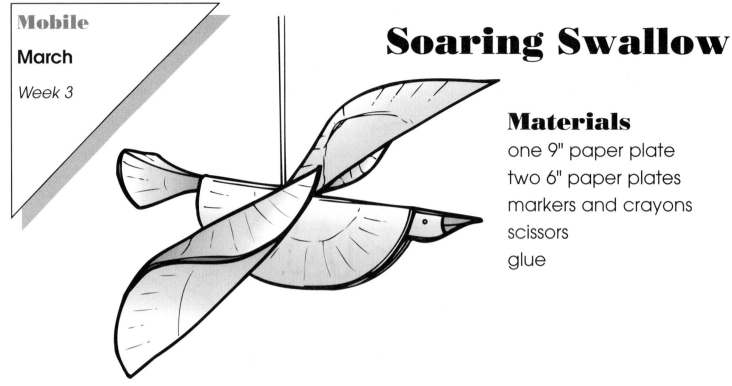

Materials

one 9" paper plate
two 6" paper plates
markers and crayons
scissors
glue

Directions

1. Color the front of the 9" plate one color and the back another color. Cut the plate in half. On each half, fold in one end at the rim approximately 1" (1.25 cm) and glue down. Glue the two folded ends together to form wings and set aside. The openings should face in opposite directions as shown. See construction guidelines on page 63.

2. Color the back of a 6" plate with one of the same colors used on the wings and set aside.

3. Use the patterns on page 63 for the tail and beak, cut out of the remaining 6" plate and color them.

4. Glue the wide end of the beak triangle to the front of the colored 6" plate at the rim. The point should be facing outward. Glue the point of the tail triangle to the same side of the plate, directly across from the beak, with the wide end pointing outward.

5. Fold the body in half and glue along the rim.

6. Press down lightly on the fold along the back to form a small flat area. Glue the wings to this area.

Variation

Attach a string to the back of the swallow and hang it outside to twirl in the breeze.

Literature Selection

Song of the Swallows
by Leo Politi
Macmillan, 1987

Selected Activity

Use this activity in your science curriculum. Have children research migration. Do any migrating animals travel through your town? Which ones? What time of year?

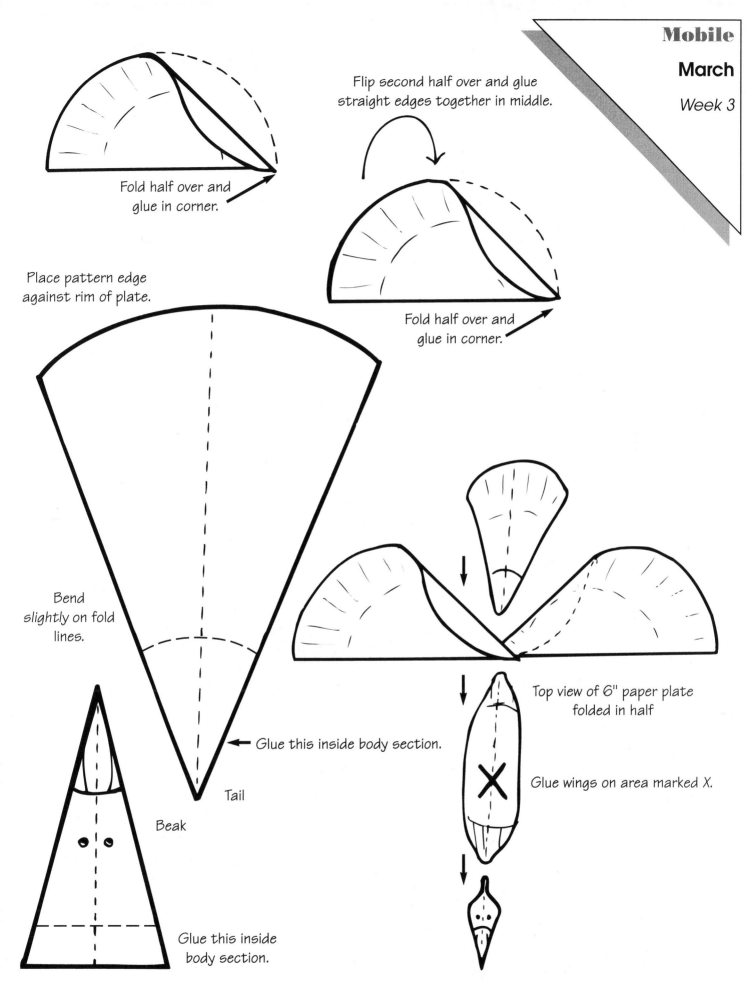

Fold half over and glue in corner.

Flip second half over and glue straight edges together in middle.

Fold half over and glue in corner.

Place pattern edge against rim of plate.

Bend slightly on fold lines.

Glue this inside body section.

Tail

Beak

Glue this inside body section.

Top view of 6" paper plate folded in half

Glue wings on area marked X.

Funny Bunny

Materials

three 6" paper plates
black and pink marker, crayon,
  paint or colored pencil
scissors
glue

Directions

1. Cut the rim from around one of the 6" plates to form a circle.

2. From the rim, cut out a round nose, two bunny ears and four round feet using the patterns on page 65.

3. Color the nose and the middle of the ears pink. Glue the nose to the center of the circle. Glue the ears to the back-top of the circle.

4. Draw on eyes, mouth and a tooth in black (patterns on page 65).

5. Glue the head to the back of the second 6" paper plate at the outer top. Attach the feet to the bottom.

6. Cut a round tail (pattern on page 65) from the center of the remaining 6" paper plate and glue it in place. (You may find that you have scraps large enough for the tail and only need two 6" plates for this project.)

Variations

1. Use cotton balls for the tail.

2. If you do not wish to make a white rabbit, color the parts in the color of your choice *before* gluing them together.

Literature Selections

The Bionic Bunny Show
by Marc Brown and Laurie Krasny Brown
Joy Street (Little Brown), 1984

Who's in Rabbit's House?
by Verna Aardema
Dial, 1977

Selected Activity

Decorate your spring or Easter bulletin board with these delightful funny bunnies. By varying the position of the head, you can have them facing right or left, or even standing up.

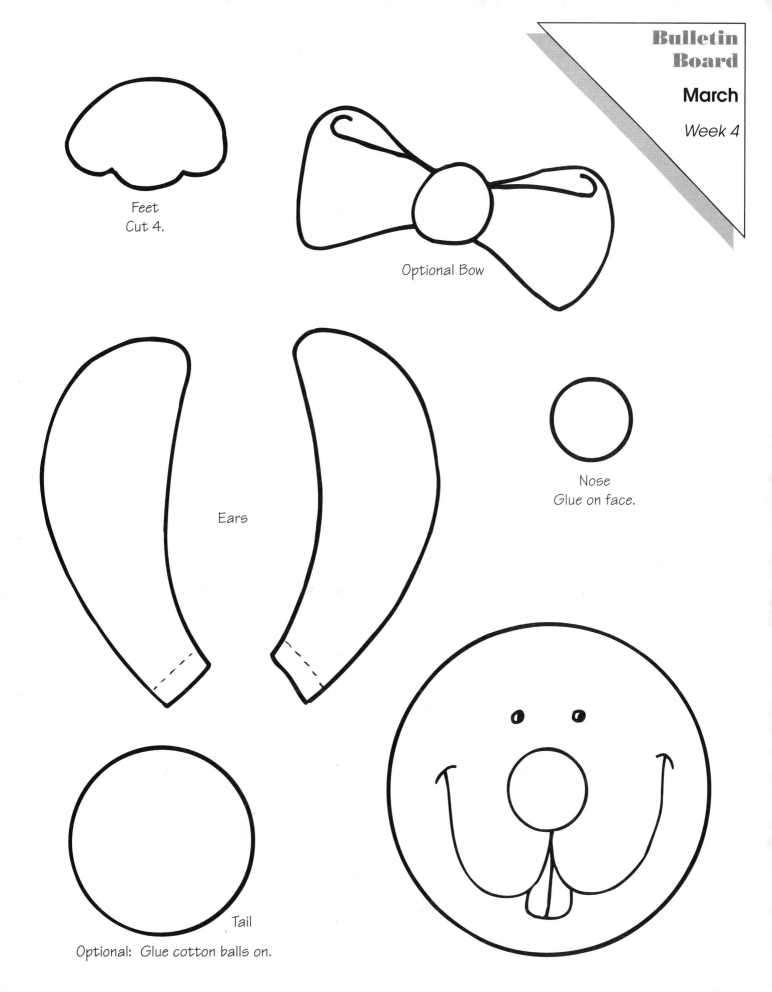

Feet
Cut 4.

Optional Bow

Ears

Nose
Glue on face.

Tail

Optional: Glue cotton balls on.

April Fools' Dog

Materials
two 9" paper plates
markers or crayons
scissors
glue

Directions
1. Copy the words *My Dog Fido*, (pattern on page 67) and paste them on the outside rim of one of the 9" plates.
2. Draw a picture in the middle of the plate of any animal EXCEPT a dog (pattern ideas on page 67). Use the second 9" plate to cut out animal features (wings, antenna, tails, etc.), and glue them to your picture.

Selected Activity
Children enjoy seeing this activity displayed on a bulletin board.

Extended Activity
You might want to extend the hilarity by creating a special take-home container for this creation. Holes poked into a cardboard box or grocery bag should provide the right amount of anticipation.

Literature Selections
It's April Fool's Day
by Steven Kroll
Holiday House, 1990

The Stupids Step Out
by Harry Allard
Houghton Mifflin, 1974

Also, *The Stupids Have a Ball* and other titles in this series.

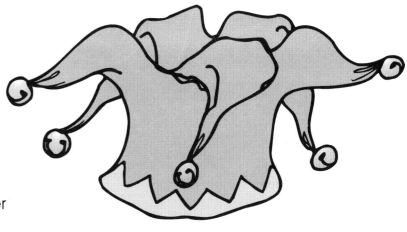

Be Kind to Animals

Materials

three 9" paper plates
markers and crayons
scissors
glue

Directions

1. Cut one of the 9" paper plates in half. Color the back green and write the words *Be Kind to Animals* on it or use the cut-out on page 70. Next, use scissors to fringe along the cut line to form sea grass blades. Bend the blades out a bit. See construction guide-lines on page 70.

2. Color the back of the second 9" plate light blue. Glue the grass onto the top of this plate, grass back to light blue front.

3. From the remaining plate or any scraps, draw a fish (or use pattern on page 69), color it and cut it out. Glue it onto the light blue plate above the grass. Cut out the *Thank You!* word balloon (pat-tern on page 69). Glue it down near the mouth of the fish.

Variation

Children can draw an animal of their choice.

Literature Selection

Crusade for Kindness: Henry Bergh and the ASPCA (grades 3-7)
by John J. Loeper
Atheneum, 1991

Selected Activity

Decorate your bulletin board with a sea full of fish! Encourage children to decorate their fish with bright col-ors, scraps of foil, glitter, stickers or anything else they think will be attractive.

68

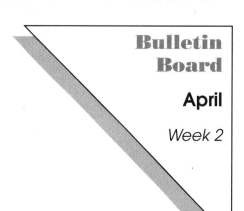

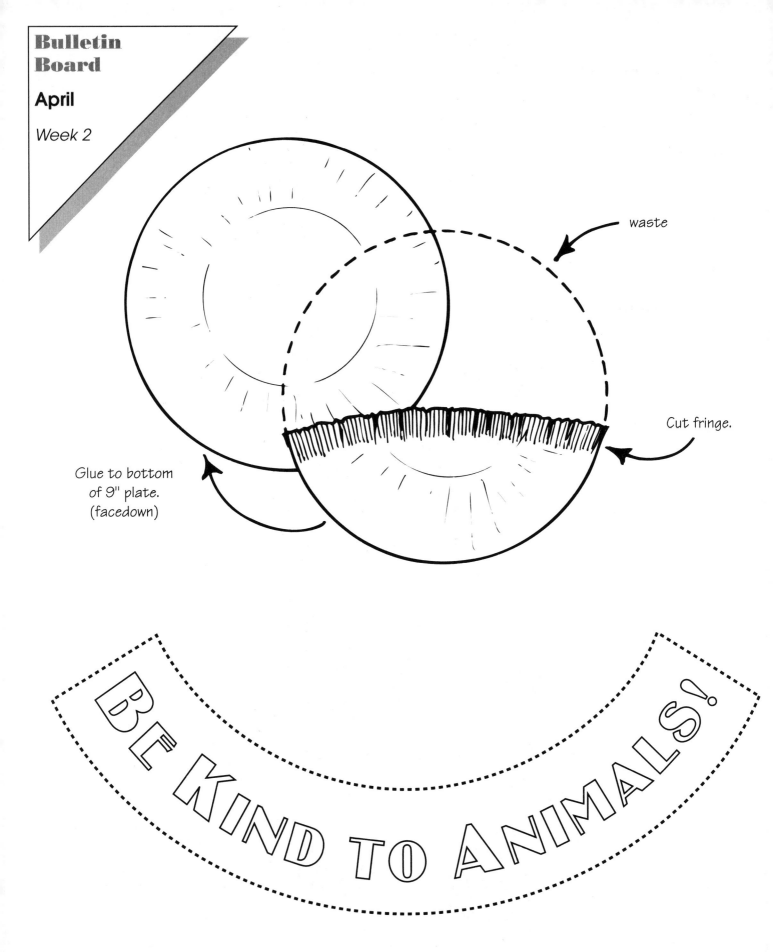

waste

Cut fringe.

Glue to bottom
of 9" plate.
(facedown)

BE KIND TO ANIMALS!

Celebrate Passover

Materials

one 9" paper plate
three 6" paper plates
markers or crayons
scissors
glue

Directions

1. Color the backs of the 9" plate and one of the 6" plates. Glue the front of the 6" plate to the center back of the 9" plate. This will be the base.

2. Copy the "Exodus from Egypt" picture (see page 72) and paste it onto the front of another 6" plate. Glue the back of this plate onto the middle of the base.

3. Color the back of the remaining 6" plate and cut a large Star of David (pattern on page 72) from the middle. Glue this plate front down onto the plate with the picture on it. (You should be able to see the drawing through the star-shaped opening.) See page 72 for construction guidelines.

Variations

1. Instead of using the picture, ask your children to draw something that means Passover to them.

2. You may wish to save time by using colored paper plates.

Literature Selection

Penny and the Four Questions
by Nancy E. Krulik
Scholastic, 1993

Selected Activity

Use this activity in your social studies curriculum. Have children find out more about the Passover holiday and celebration.

Exodus from Egypt

Star of David

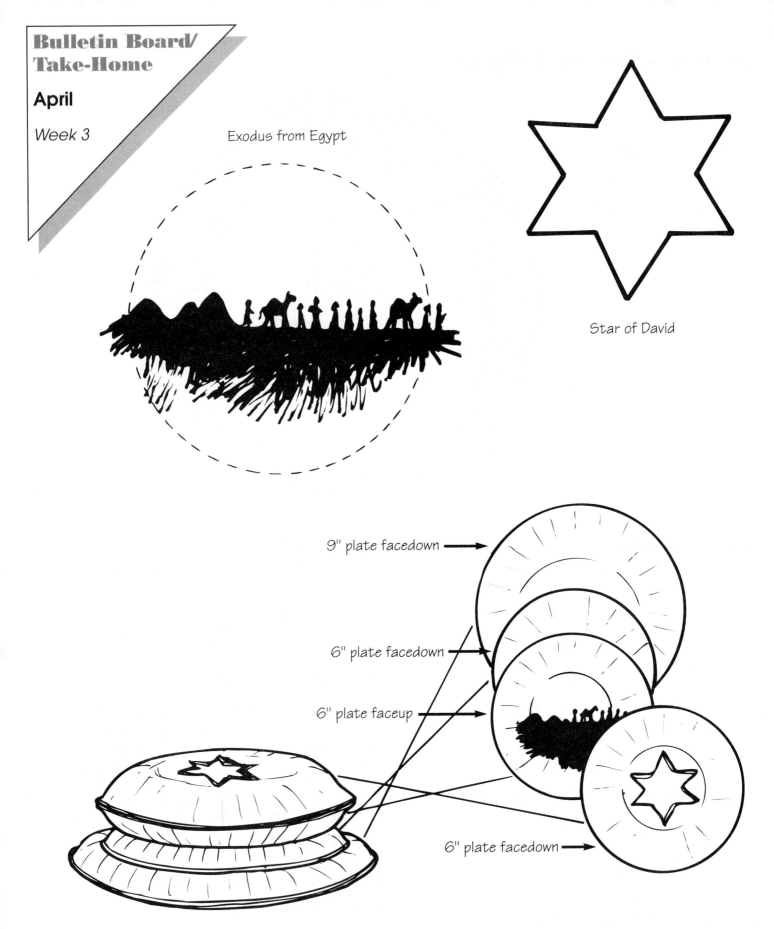

9" plate facedown →

6" plate facedown →

6" plate faceup →

6" plate facedown →

In Like a Lion

Materials

one 9" paper plate
markers or crayons
scissors
glue

Directions

1. Color the front of a 9" plate yellow. Copy the lion's face on page 74, color it and glue it in the center.
2. Fringe the outer rim of the plate all the way around to resemble a lion's mane. Separate the fringes, and curl some of them around your fingers.

Literature Selections

Johnny Lion's Rubber Boots
by Edith T. Hurd
HarperCollins, 1972

*Puddle Wonderful:
   Poems to Welcome Spring*
selected by Bobbi Katz
Random House, 1992

Selected Activity

Decorate your bulletin board with these delightful faces, or cut out eye holes and add ear loops of yarn to wear them as masks.

Extended Activity

These lions can start a discussion of spring (and the old saying, "In like a lion and out like a lamb") or they might lead to an investigation of lion life and habitat, or they could prompt dramatic play based on the many lions in literature, or they might inspire a session of creative writing. Be prepared to let these lions lead you into lots of learning!

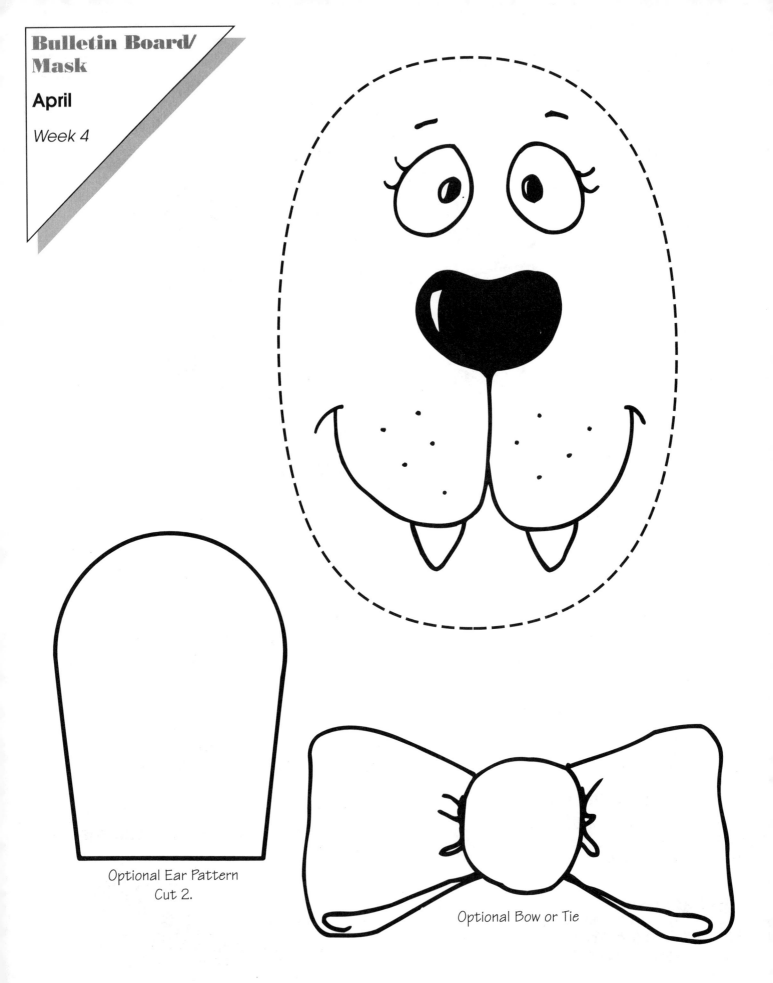

Optional Ear Pattern
Cut 2.

Optional Bow or Tie

Cinco de Mayo Shaker

Materials

three 9" paper plates
beans or rice
markers or crayons
scissors
glue

Directions

1. Color the backs of two 9" plates in a festive color (or colors). Place a handful of beans or rice on one plate; then glue the other on top, front to front.

2. Cut the brim and top of the sombrero from the rim of the remaining plate (patterns on page 76). Color and glue it to the center of the shaker.

3. From the scraps of the third plate, cut out and color 12 flowers (patterns on pages 76 and 77).

4. Glue the flowers on the shaker in twos (one on top of another) all around the rim of the shaker. Bend the petals up on the top flowers.

Variations

1. Flowers could be cut from construction paper or tissue paper.

2. Instead of gluing the plates together, use a hole punch to punch evenly spaced holes in the rim of the plates. Sew them together with yarn. (Beans work better as filler for this method.)

Literature Selection

Cinco de Mayo
by Janet Riehecky
Children's Press, 1993

Selected Activity

Research this holiday. Where does it come from? Who celebrates it and how? What is the event it commemorates?

75

Flowers
Cut 12.

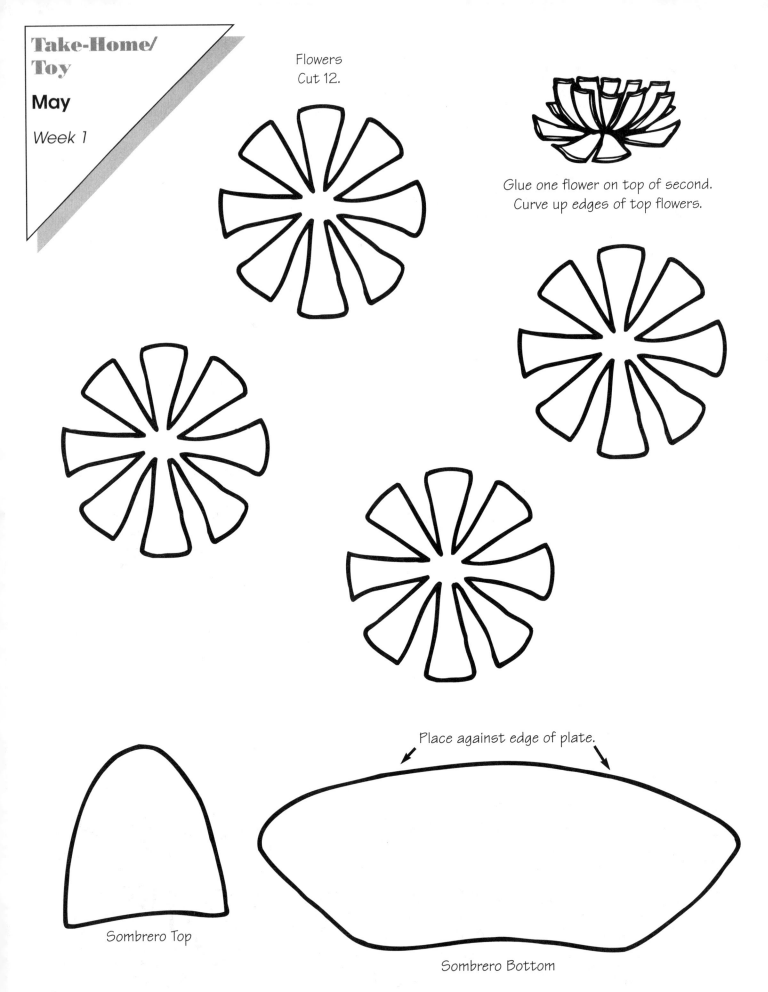

Glue one flower on top of second.
Curve up edges of top flowers.

Place against edge of plate.

Sombrero Top

Sombrero Bottom

Mother's Day Butterfly

Materials

two 9" paper plates
markers or crayons
scissors
glue

Directions

1. Color the back of one 9" plate in your mother's favorite color. On the front write a special message and sign your name. Set this base plate aside.

2. Cut and color butterfly wings from the second plate (pattern on page 80). Glue the wings to the base plate, back to back and slightly toward the top. At the bottom, between the wings, write, *Happy Mother's Day*.

3. From the scraps, cut out and color a body, head and antenna (patterns on page 79). Draw a face on the head. Glue the body to the wings. Glue the head to the body. Glue the antenna to the top of the head.

Variations

1. This project could be used to honor a favorite female.

2. Preprinted plates can be used for the base and the wings.

3. Put potpourri on another 9" plate. Glue this plate onto the base plate of the butterfly (front to front) with the potpourri enclosed. Poke holes in the plates to let the fragrance escape.

Literature Selections

The Mother's Day Mice
by Eve Bunting
Clarion, 1986

Mother's Day Sandwich
by Jillian Wynot
Orchard Books, 1990

78

Antenna

Head

If you do not wish to use this project for Mother's Day, you can create a dazzling bulletin board by filling it with dozens and dozens of your students' butterflies. Research butterflies for exact wing coloration and pattern, and have your students try to copy the originals. Students can also decorate their butterflies with glitter, stickers, tissue paper, foil, confetti, yarn, etc. There are many possibilities.

Extended Activity

Commercial butterfly kits are available; your class might like to try "growing" a butterfly this year.

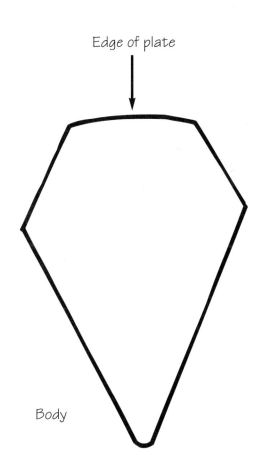

Edge of plate

Body

79

TLC10039 Copyright © Teaching & Learning Company, Carthage, IL 62321

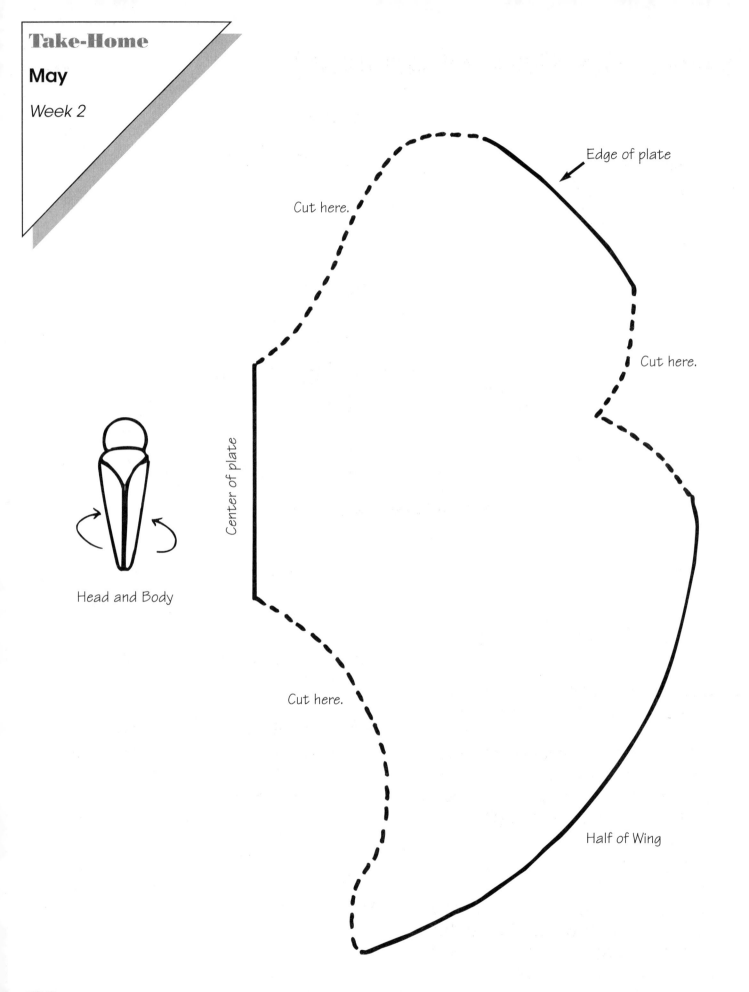

Edge of plate

Cut here.

Cut here.

Center of plate

Cut here.

Half of Wing

Head and Body

Victoria Day (Canada)

Materials

three 9" paper plates
markers or crayons
scissors
glue

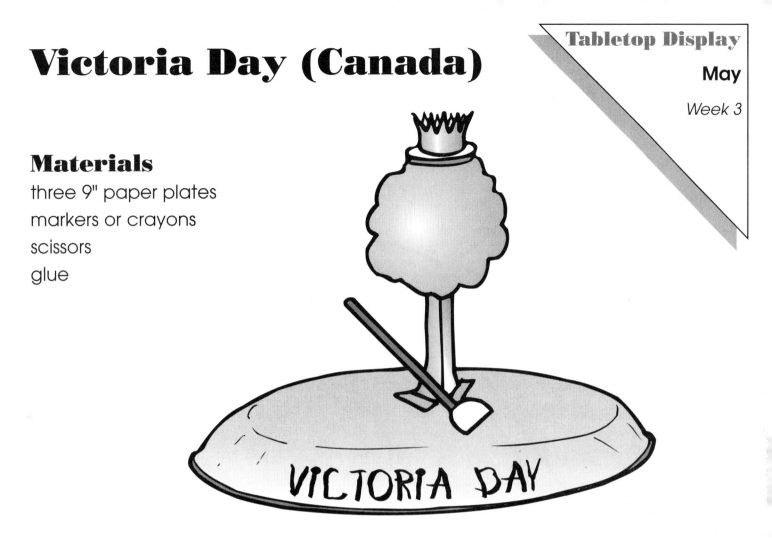

Directions

1. Color the back of one of the 9" plates to look like grass. Write the words *Victoria Day* around the rim.

2. Cut out and color the hoe, tree trunk and leaves from the second paper plate (patterns on page 82). Bend the trunk in half. Glue the trunk tab to the center of the grass plate. Next, bend up the bottom of the hoe and glue it in place.

3. Cut a 4¹/₂" (11 cm) long piece of rim from the third 9" plate. Color it yellow. Cut "Vs" along one side. Roll it into a crown and glue the ends in place. See construction guidelines on page 82.

4. Cut out a small circle base (pattern on page 82) to set the crown on and glue to the top of the tree.

5. Glue the crown on top of the circle base on top of the tree.

Literature Selection

Check your school or local library for age-appropriate materials on Queen Victoria and the celebration.

Selected Activity

Celebrate Victoria Day in your classroom. Use this project to decorate your tables.

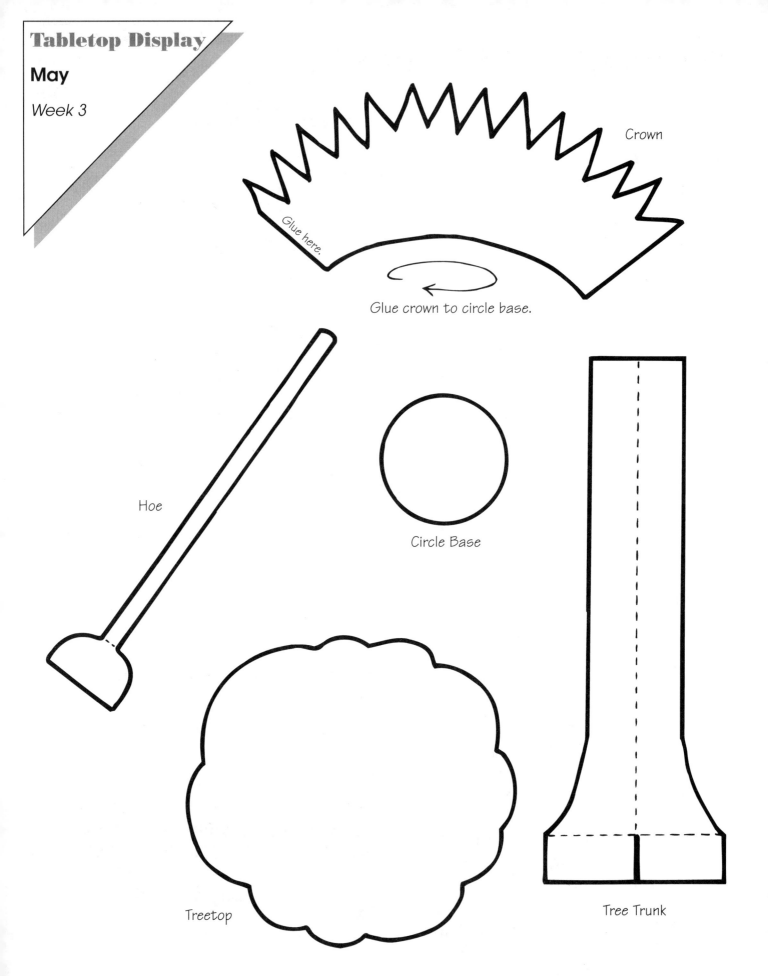

Crown

Glue here.

Glue crown to circle base.

Hoe

Circle Base

Treetop

Tree Trunk

"Spring"y Flowers

Materials

two 9" paper plates
one 6" paper plate
markers or crayons
scissors
glue

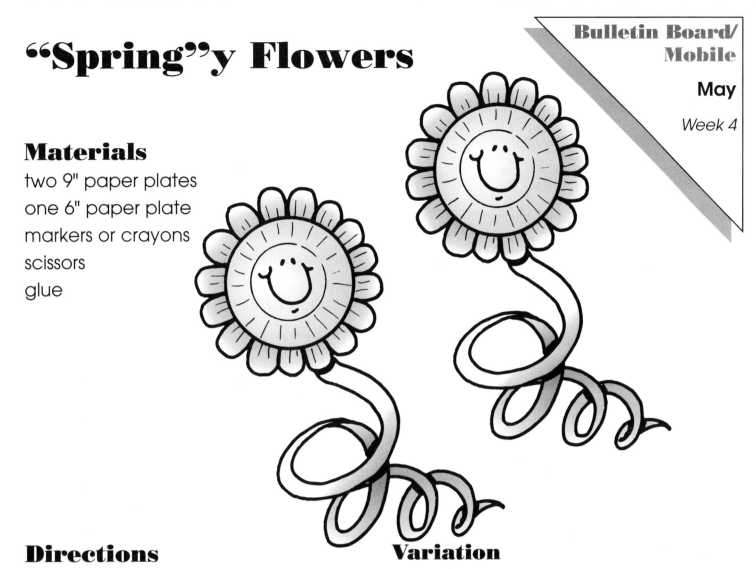

Directions

1. Color the back of the 6" plate yellow and draw a face on it (pattern on page 84). Set this plate aside.

2. Color the inside of one of the 9" plates your favorite color. Cut the outer rim into the shape of flower petals (patterns on page 84).

3. Glue the 6" plate, front down, onto the middle of the petal plate.

4. Cut a circle out of the center of the second 9" plate. Color the circle green and cut it into a spiral. Glue one end of the spiral to the back of your flower. Let the glue dry before you handle your flower.

Variation

Do not glue the face at the top. Slip in a packet of flower seeds and give this project as a gift.

Literature Selection

The Reason for a Flower
by Ruth Heller
Grosset & Dunlap, 1983

Selected Activity

Decorate your bulletin board with these "spring"y flowers. Pin at the top and let the spiral stems hang free. Attach yarn to the top of your flower, and hang it from the ceiling for a mobile.

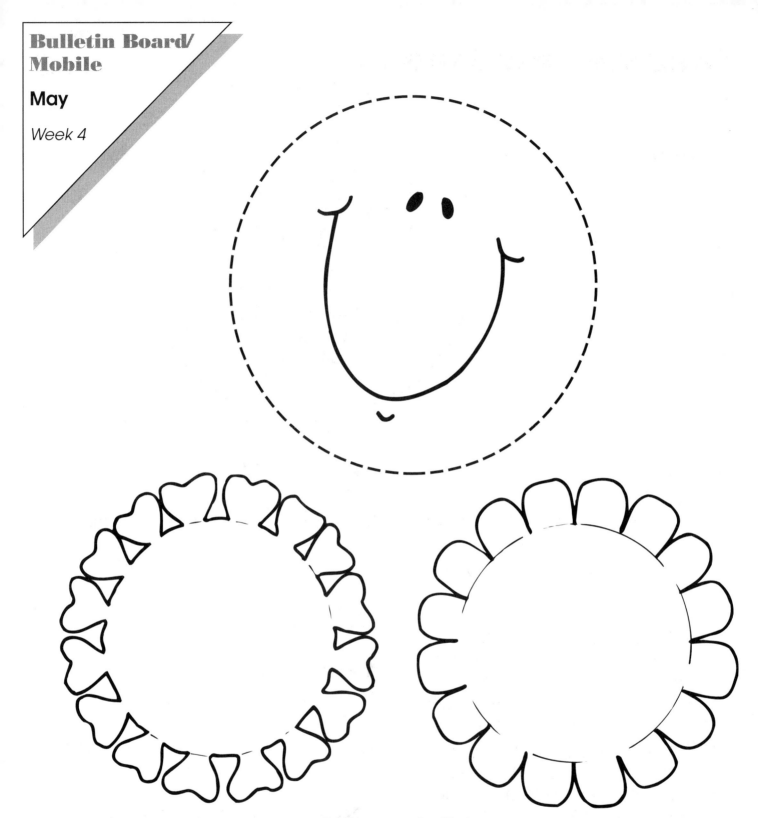

Petal patterns for 9" plate

Number One Dad

Materials

two 9" paper plates
one 6" paper plate
markers or crayons
scissors
paper
glue
pencil

Directions

1. Color the back of one of the 9" plates in your Dad's favorite color.

2. Color the front of the 6" plate. Write the number symbol (#) on the plate to the left of the center.

3. Cut out and color a paper ribbon from the second 9" plate (pattern on page 86). Glue the end without the V-shape cut-out to the lower back of the 6" plate. Write the word *DAD* on the ribbon.

4. Copy and cut out the numeral one (pattern on page 86) and glue it onto a paper plate scrap. Make a pedestal* from paper and glue it to the back of the numeral. Glue the back of the pedestal to the front middle of the 6" plate.

5. Glue the back of the 6" plate to the upper middle of the back of the colored 9" plate.

*A pedestal can be a paper spring, strip of paper folded into a cube, a piece of sponge, anything that will raise the object. See "Tips and Suggestions" (pages vii-ix) at the front of the book.

Variations

1. To save time, you could use pre-printed plates.

2. This project can be used to honor a favorite male figure.

Literature Selections

Hooray for Father's Day
by Marjorie Weinman Sharmat
Holiday House, 1987

A Perfect Father's Day
by Eve Bunting
Clarion, 1991

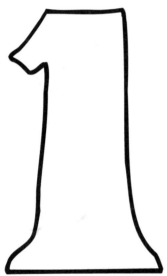

Selected Activity

If you do not wish to use this project for Father's Day, you can delete the word *DAD* from the ribbon and substitute whatever may be appropriate (super student, local team, favorite book, etc.). Turn the project into a bulletin board display featuring the number one of your choice.

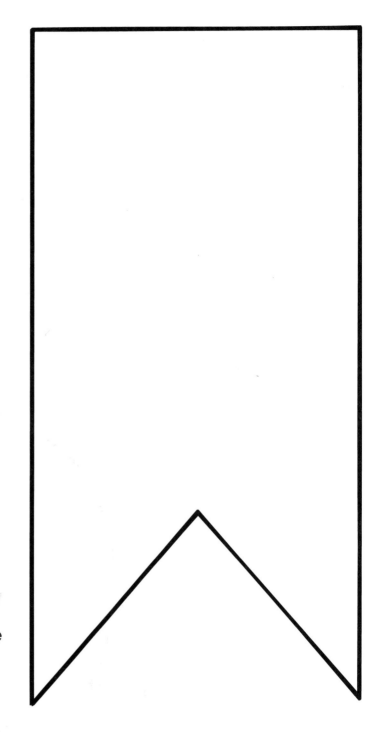

Sammy the Snake

Materials

one 9" paper plate
markers or crayons
scissors
glue

Directions

1. Cut out a head using the pattern on page 88 from the middle of the 9" paper plate. Color the head and draw a snake face on it.

2. Cut the rim of the paper plate into two pieces. Use them to form a long tail by gluing two ends together. Color the tail and glue the head onto one end. See construction guidelines on page 88.

3. Make a tongue out of any left-over scraps using the pattern on page 88. Color and glue it to the head.

Variation

Make your snake super snazzy! Decorate with glitter, stickers, yarn, macaroni, whatever suits your situation.

Literature Selections

Small Green Snake
by Libba Moore Gray
Orchard Books, 1994

The Snake Lover's Diary
by Barbara Brenner
Young Scott Books, 1970

Selected Activity

Use Sammy to study the sound of the letter *S*. If you desire, you can glue the rims together so that they form the letter *S*.

If you have students who like to garden, or if you have an outdoor garden at school, you can use this project to scare off birds. Place it on the ground between the plants. It really works!

Create a bulletin board garden with the "Spring"y Flowers (page 83) and these snakes.

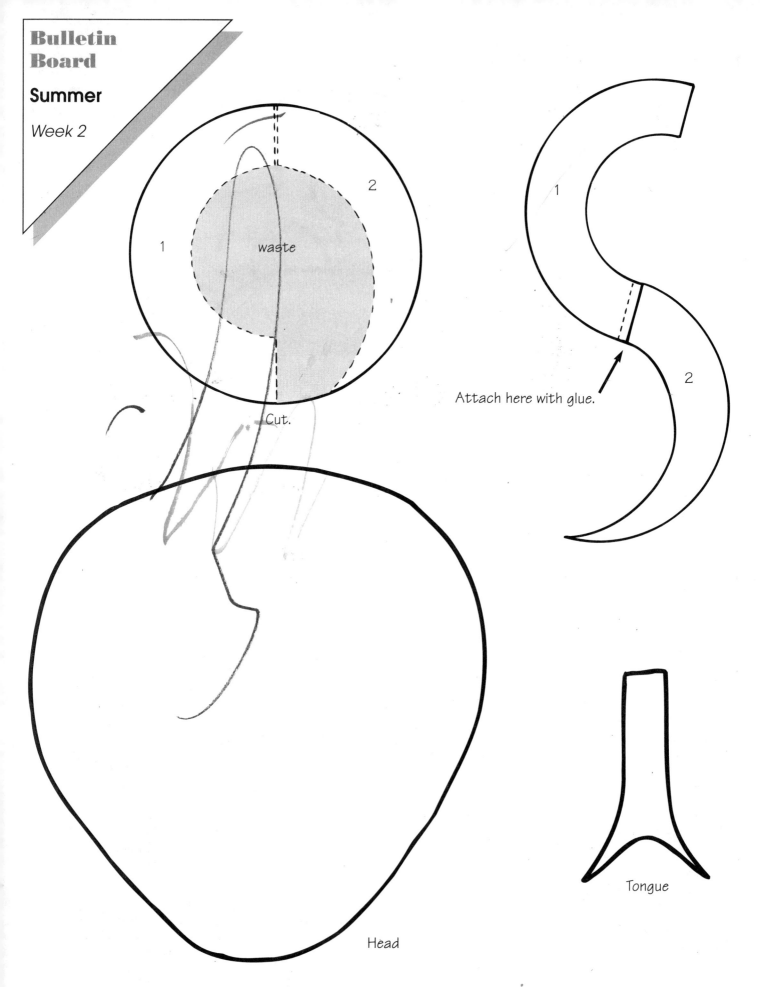

2

1

waste

Cut.

1

2

Attach here with glue.

Head

Tongue

Ice Cream Cone

Materials

one 9" paper plate (makes 2)
cotton batting
markers or crayons
yarn
scissors
glue

Directions

1. Cut the paper plate in half. Color the back to look like an ice cream cone.
2. Bend the plate, rim side up, to form a cone. Glue the ends together.
3. Attach yarn to each side to form a loop for hanging.
4. Fill the cone with cotton.

Variations

This project could become a variety of things: a cornucopia for Thanksgiving, a treat holder for birthday parties, a candy holder for Halloween, etc. See page 90 for ideas.

Literature Selection

The Tutti Frutti Case
by Harry Allard
Prentice-Hall, 1975

Selected Activity

Ask children how they think the ice cream cone came about. Have them investigate the true origin of the ice cream cone. It's an interesting story!

Liberty Bell

Materials

two 9" paper plates
markers or crayons
scissors
glue

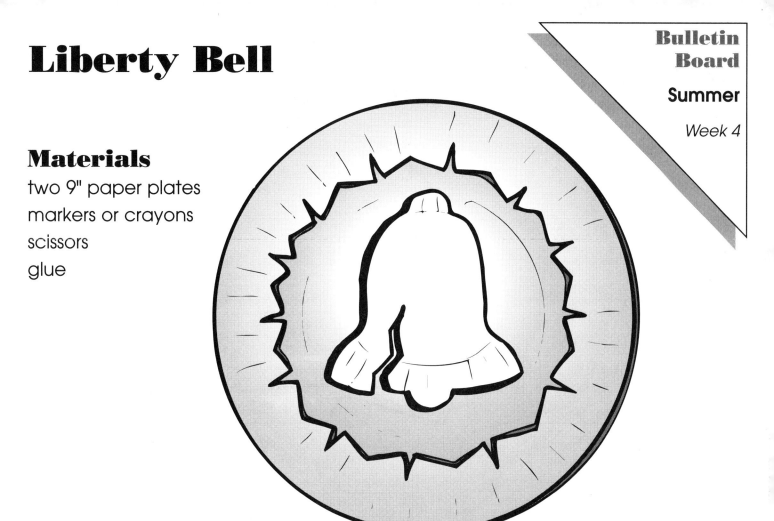

Directions

1. Make a large cut-out in a star-burst (pattern on page 92) around the inside of the rim of a 9" plate. Leave the rim intact. Color the back of the rim red.

2. Color the front of the second plate dark blue. Glue the front of the red rim to the front of the blue plate.

3. Copy the Liberty Bell shape (pattern on page 92) and glue to a large scrap. Cut out around the outline of the bell. Make a pedestal from paper and attach to the back of the bell. Glue the back of the pedestal to the middle of the blue plate.

Variation

Use glitter to make this project really sparkle!

Literature Selection

Henry's Fourth of July
by Holly Keller
Greenwillow, 1985

Selected Activity

Use the Liberty Bells to create an attractive bulletin board display. Alternate the colors (make some with red rims and blue plates, others with blue rims and red plates) for an interesting effect.

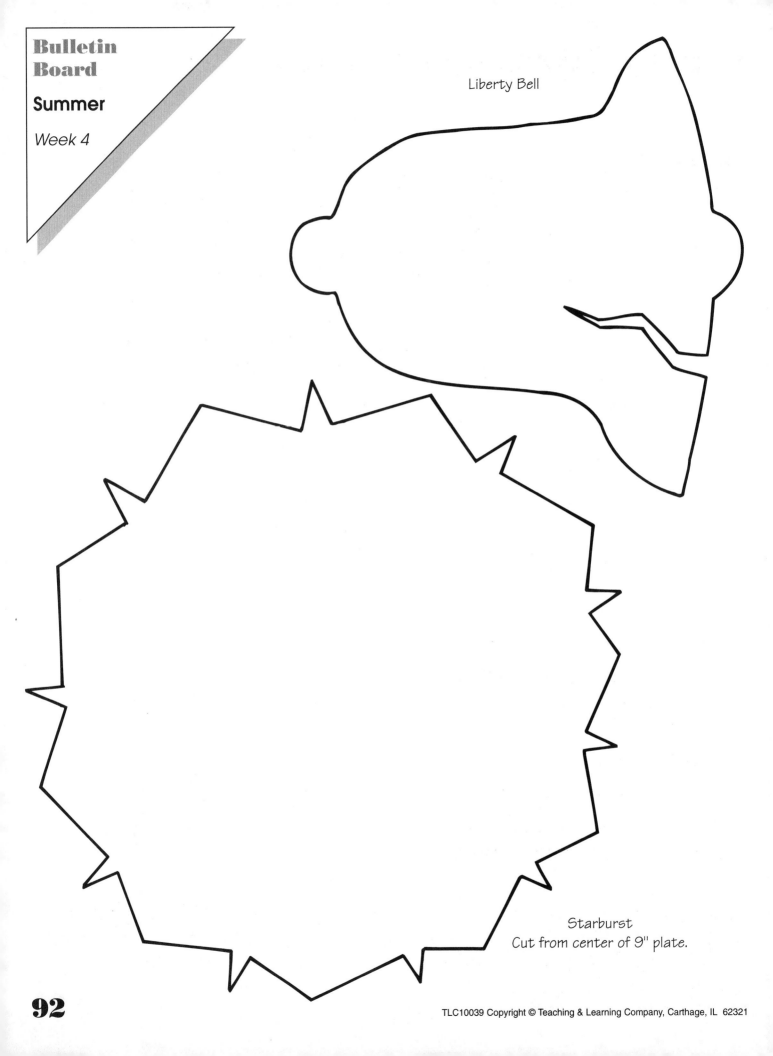

Liberty Bell

Starburst
Cut from center of 9" plate.

Happy Birthday Crown

Materials

three 9" paper plates
markers or crayons
scissors
glue

Directions

1. Copy the crown pattern (page 94) and glue to the middle of two of the paper plates. Cut out and color. Glue the ends of the two strips together to form a longer strip.

2. From the scraps and remaining plate, color and cut out a headband (pattern on page 94) and jewels to decorate the crown. Glue these into place.

Variation

Use glitter, scraps of foil or tissue paper or stickers to decorate this crown. You might even want to write the birthday child's name in glitter glue.

Selected Activity

This project can also be used as part of a costume for a play or to award an outstanding achievement.

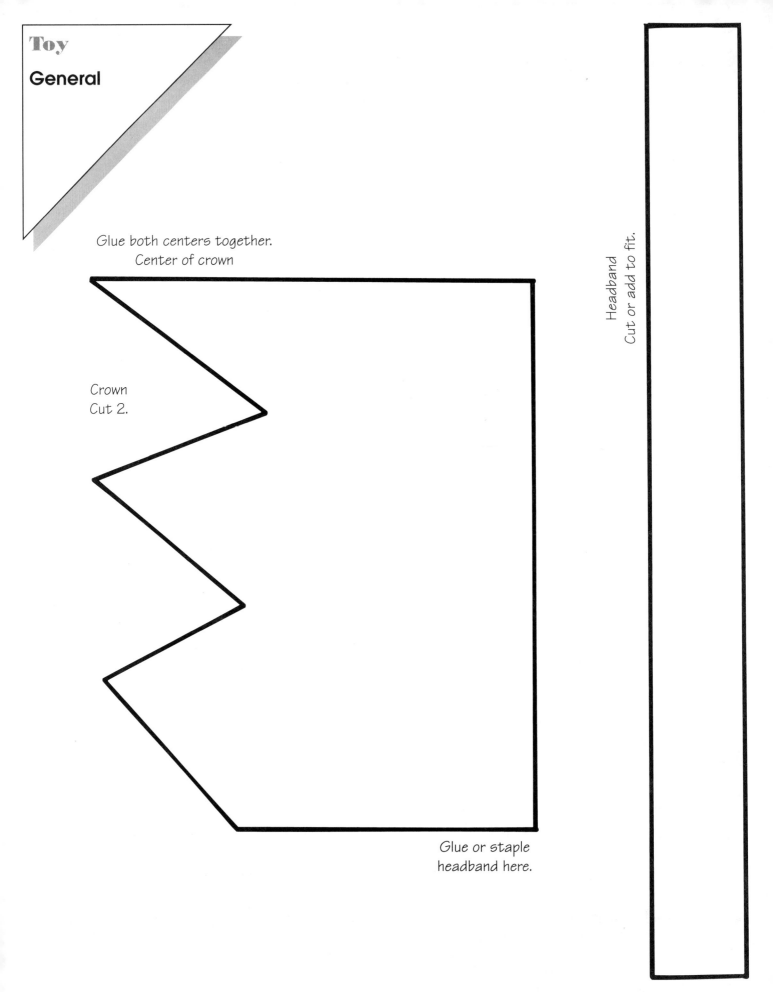

Glue both centers together.
Center of crown

Crown
Cut 2.

Glue or staple
headband here.

Headband
Cut or add to fit.

94

Blooming Flower

Materials

three 9" paper plates
six 6" paper plates
markers or crayons
scissors
glue

Directions

1. Color the back of a 9" and a 6" paper plate in the colors of your choice. Poke a ¹/₂" (1.25 cm) hole in the center of the 6" plate. Glue the 6" plate to the 9" plate, front to back. This will be the base. Set it aside.

2. Color the back of a 9" plate green. Roll it into a tight flower stem. Glue the edge to hold it shut. Make four 1" (2.5 cm) cuts into the top of the stem and bend back. These will hold the flower.

3. Put glue into the hole on the base plate and place the uncut end of the stem into the hole. Hold in place for a few seconds while the glue dries.

4. Cut and color leaves from the remaining 9" plate and glue them to the stem. Bend the tips outward.

5. Color the fronts and backs of four of the remaining 6" plates. Cut a "V," from rim to center, in each one. Fold and glue to create cones in varying sizes. Cut petals around the rims of the cones and bend them out slightly. Glue these cones onto the top of the stem with the largest one on the bottom and the smallest one on the top.

6. With the remaining 6" plate, cut out a small rectangle lengthwise, not too tightly, and glue one end into the center of the flower. Fringe the other end and curl fringes outward.

See construction guidelines on page 96.

Variation

You may want to present this craft in two days.

Selected Activity

This project can be used as a gift (for a birthday, Mother's Day, going-away or special event). Several of them in a single base can make a bouquet. For a long-stemmed version, eliminate the base plate and double the length of the stem.

Glue flower here.

Yellow Fringe

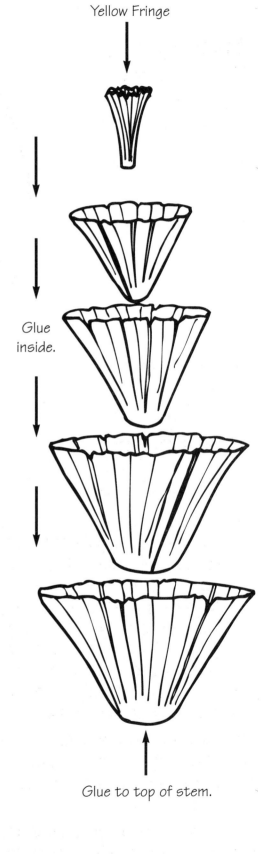

Glue inside.

Roll plate tightly.

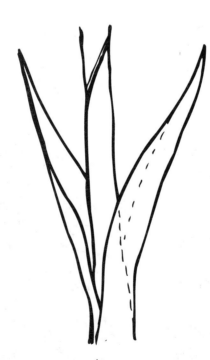

Leaves

Glue to top of stem.

Sunny Congratulations

Materials

two 9" paper plates
one 6" paper plate
markers or crayons
scissors

Directions

1. Color the back of one of the 9" plates light blue.

2. Around the rim of the 6" plate, cut "V"s to resemble sunbeams. (Save the cut-outs.) Color the sun yellow and draw on a face (pattern on page 98). Glue the sun to the bottom half of the light blue plate. Turn the scrap "V"s upside down and glue them between and behind the sunbeams to make more beams.

3. Cut the remaining 9" plate in half. Copy the banner (pattern on page 98) and glue it to the half plate. Cut out.

4. Put a dot of glue at each end of the banner, and glue above the sun on the light blue plate.

Variation

Personalize the banner by writing a student's name on it.

Selected Activity

Create a bright bulletin board by displaying these sunny projects.

Tricky Triceratops

Materials

three 9" paper plates
two 6" paper plates
markers or crayons
scissors
glue

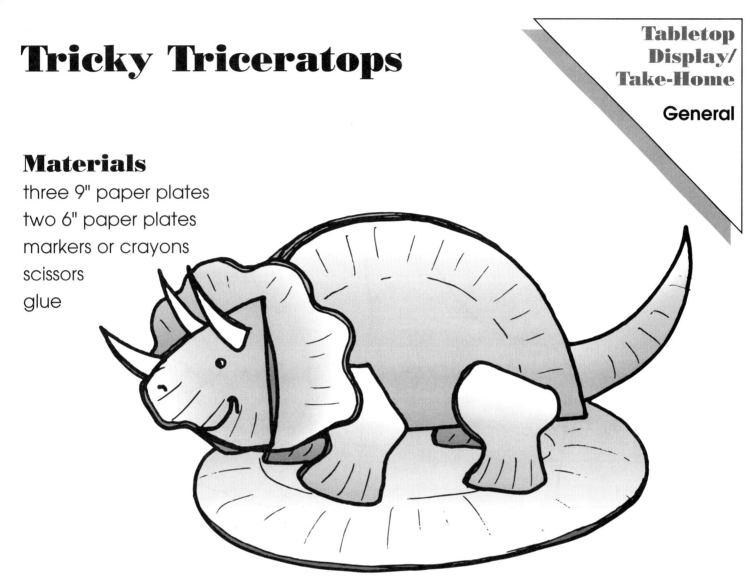

Directions

1. Color the back of one of the 9" plates green or brown to resemble the ground. This will be the base. Set it aside.

2. Ask your students to decide what color they would like to make their dinosaur. Color the back of a 9" plate this color. Fold the plate in half, front to front and cut about 1/4" (.6 cm), in a diagonal, off of one side. Set aside.

3. From the remaining 9" plate, cut out legs from the middle and a tail (patterns on page 100) from the rim. Color these pieces.

4. From the 6" plates, color and cut out the neck piece (pattern on page 101). Form the head (pattern on page 101) by folding one of the plates in half and shape with scissors. Cut out and color the three horns (pattern on page 101).

5. Glue the legs to the body and bend outward at the bottom to form feet. Glue on the tail, neck piece, head and horns. Glue your triceratops to the base at the feet.

Selected Activity

This project can be used as part of a science curriculum.

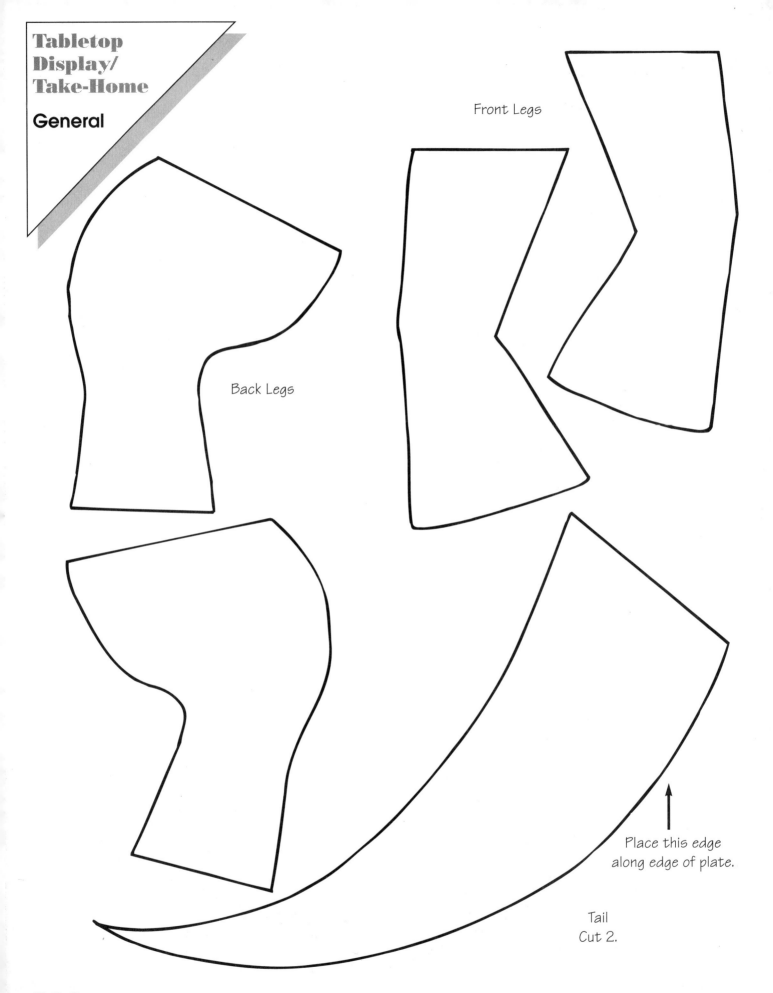

Front Legs

Back Legs

Place this edge
along edge of plate.

Tail
Cut 2.

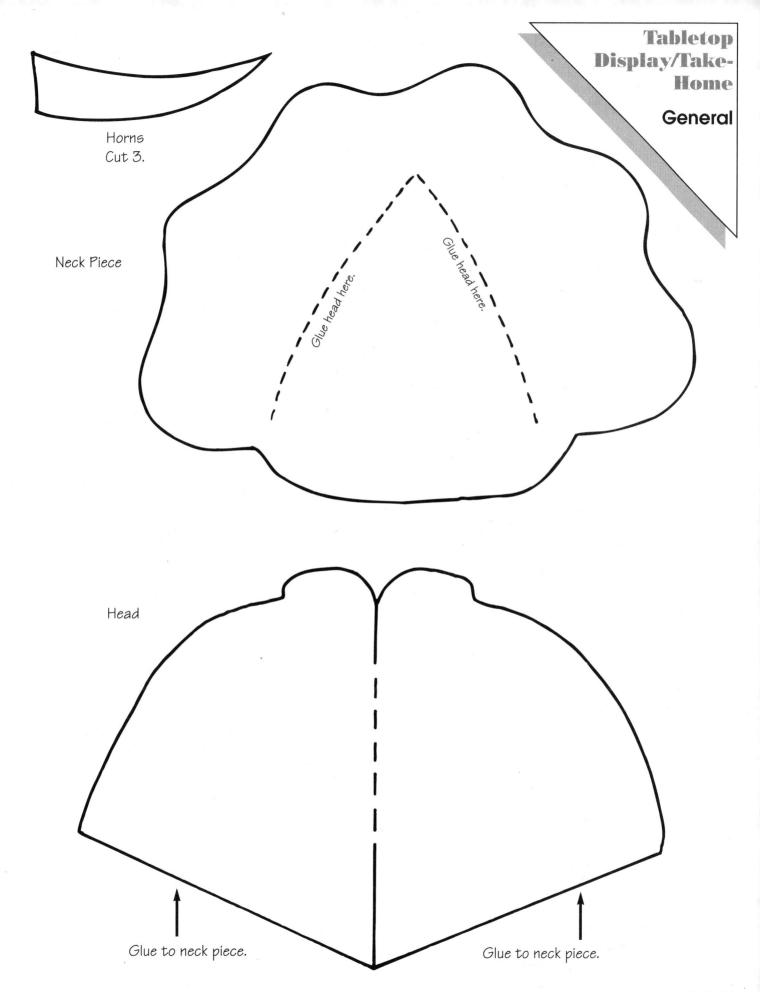

Horns
Cut 3.

Neck Piece

Glue head here.

Glue head here.

Head

Glue to neck piece.

Glue to neck piece.

Field of Flowers

Materials
three 9" paper plates
markers or crayons
scissors
glue

Directions
1. Cut one plate into thirds, making the inside cut of the top third look like clouds and the inside cut of the bottom third look like grass. Color, on the back, green for the grass and leave the clouds white.

2. Color the inside of the second plate light blue. Glue the clouds to the top, front to front, and the grass to the bottom, also front to front.

3. From the scraps and the remaining plate, color and cut out flowers and butterflies. Glue the flowers to the middle of the plate and the butterflies around the rim.

Selected Activity
This project can be used as a get well, welcome, birthday or congratulations card.

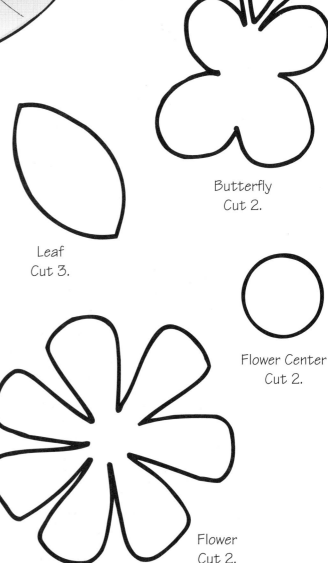

Butterfly
Cut 2.

Leaf
Cut 3.

Flower Center
Cut 2.

Flower
Cut 2.

102